Captain E. Raymond Hepper's
Great War Diary 1916-1919

E. Raymond Hepper as a junior officer in the
West Yorkshire Regiment, 1915.

Captain E. Raymond Hepper's
GREAT WAR DIARY 1916-1919

A battalion of the West Yorkshire Regiment on the Somme during the First World War

Edited by F. Nigel Hepper

HAYLOFT PUBLISHING LTD
CUMBRIA

First published by Hayloft 2011

Hayloft Publishing Ltd, South Stainmore, Kirkby Stephen,
Cumbria, CA17 4DJ

tel: 07971 352473
email: books@hayloft.eu
web: www.hayloft.eu

ISBN 1 904524 81 8

CAP data for this title are available from the British Library

Designed, printed and bound in the EU

Papers used by Hayloft are natural, recyclable products made from wood grown in
sustainable forest. The manufacturing processes conform to the environmental
regulations of the country of origin.

*This book is dedicated to the memory of my father and my uncle,
and to the generation of those who fought in the Great War,
many millions of whom lived in appalling conditions,
and were wounded or killed.*

Certificate of moral character during the past four years. If the candidate college, or other educational establishment during any portion of the period the signed by the head of the establishment, otherwise it may be signed by a respe near relative or connection), e.g., the minister of the parish or other local clergy a senior officer of the Army or Navy who has been well acquainted with the candidate life during the period.

If the above-mentioned person cannot certify for the whole period of four years, for the period not covered by the first should be signed by a similar person.

I hereby certify to the good moral character of _Edward R. Hepper_

for the last _20 years_

Signature ....

‡Rank, office or occupation ....

Date .... Address ....

To be filled in when the above certificate does not cover four years.

I hereby certify to the good moral character of ....

from .... to ....

Signature _James E. Bedford_

‡Rank, office or occupation _Lord Mayor of Leeds_

Date .... Address _Town Hall Leeds_

‡Evidence that the candidate has obtained a good standard of education.
If the candidate has :—
(a) obtained a leaving or qualifying certificate as required of a candidate for to the Royal Military College under the regulations in force up to 1st April, Certificate should be attached :
(b) qualified at an Army Entrance Examination, the date of examination should
(c) passed the matriculation examination of a University, or a test accepted in lie the Certificate should be attached.
Failing one of the above, the following certificate must be signed by the Headmaster secondary school or other competent educational authority.

I certify from personal knowledge that _Edward R Hepper_ has
a good standard of education.

J Osborne Edward M A
Headmaster of Leeds Grammar

State here educational position, e.g.,
Head of a College or School, etc.

†Here state whether the Head of School or College, Minister of Parish or other local clergyman, or Magist

The Commanding Officer recommending the candidate will sign the following certificate :—

I certify that I am well acquainted with _Edward Raymond Hepper_
and can recommend him as a suitable candidate in all respects for appointment to a commission in the Regular Army for the period of the war in the rank of _2nd Lieut_

C. Pollard Maj
Leeds Bn

Raymond's enlistment papers signed by James Bedford, 1914, with kind permission of the National Archives.

Contents

Foreword

On 9 June 1920, HM King George V formally opened the Imperial War Museum in its original location of the Crystal Palace. In his speech at the event, the politician and industrialist Sir Alfred Mond declared that, 'it is hoped to make [the collection] so complete that every individual, man or woman, sailor, soldier, airman or civilian who contributed, however obscurely, to the final result, may be able to find in these galleries an example or illustration of the sacrifice he made or the work he did, and in the archives some record of it.' This is a tradition that we have kept close to our hearts in the wars and conflicts that have followed.

Today, the Imperial War Museum has an unparalleled and unique collection covering all aspects of twentieth and twenty-first century conflict involving Britain, the Commonwealth and other former empire countries. It has benefited hugely from the kindness and generosity of strangers; ex-members of the Services and a wide-range of members of the general public who have passed to us their books, writings and memorabilia that might have otherwise been lost to history. The Document collection today stands at over 17,500 collections of letters, diaries and memoirs which effectively record the toil and sacrifices of over 17,500 individuals.

Of the many thousands of collections that the Imperial War Museum holds, Edward Raymond Hepper's diary is a fine example of the kind of personal war record that we are most keen to preserve. The account of his experiences with the 17th Battalion West Yorkshire Regiment continues to be of considerable interest to historians studying the life of a regimental officer on the Western Front during the First World War, and remains an important part of our ever-expanding holdings on the conflict.

This publication of Hepper's war diary makes the account even more valuable by its inclusion of biographical information, historical notes and a most useful index. It will undoubtedly prove of great benefit to future historians.

Anthony Richards
Head of Documents and Sound
Imperial War Museum

*Raymond's family and their car, registration number U6, in about 1913.
Raymond's mother, Gertrude, in the driving seat, with her father (James
Bedford) and his wife in the rear seats. Raymond's father, Edward, is
standing.*

Introduction

By F. Nigel Hepper
(Raymond's second son, born 13 March 1929, Leeds)

THE original diary in a fat, fool's-cap, leather-bound ledger was micro-filmed by the Imperial War Museum (IWM) in 1978 and the manuscript returned to my brother John in Leeds. The whereabouts of the ledger after John's death in 1991 is obscure but I still hope it will turn up as it is a great loss, not only of the text but of the numerous original photographs and hand-drawn maps.

In the meantime, I have photocopied the entire microfilm thanks to the IWM, and transcribed it at my home in Richmond. As the original pages were fool's-cap they are longer than current A4 size so many of the earlier photocopies cut off the lower lines which I copied manually during a later visit to IWM. However, Mr Anthony Richard of the staff, later showed me how to reduce the size of the page in order to include all the text for the remainder of the pages which were kindly provided *gratis* by IWM. The microfilm text is shown up on a machine page by page, so I noted the num-ber of the 'frame', and added a selection of these numbers to the Summary of the Diary below.

Although Father's handwriting is neat and tidy, many words are difficult to read accurately, especially when photocopied from the microfilm. Place-names needed to be verified from published maps and some may still be wrong. As mentioned above, the original photographs and maps did not reproduce well from the microfilm, with very few exceptions. This is a great pity since my father included many original aerial photographs which he had used for intelligence interpretation (a new discipline which he pio-neered) for the Somme operations. One of the maps, presumably his, included here was from an air photo dated 12-6-17 (i.e. 12 June 1917) based at the scale of 1:20,000. A couple of smaller ones were also probably his.

I have also included my outline maps of the British battlefields in France and Belgium, with place-names mentioned in the diary. These names I have double-checked as some transcriptions were guesswork from Father's hand-writing; but others I have not located, some were ephemeral names of trenches and other earthworks. Note that several place-name spellings have since changed e.g. Poperinghe is now Poperinge; and Ypres is Ieper. I have included some photographs of French places before and after war damage. Also included are my own drawings of plants and animals mentioned in the text as Father was a keen naturalist, as shown below. In spite of the dreadful conditions on the battlefields, he retained his humour and interest in places of culture.

The **place-names** and **personal names** have been **highlighted** by me in this transcript. These and the military units mentioned have been indexed alphabetically. I have inserted a few subheadings here and there; the dates are in full e.g. Feb. 3 is now entered as 3 February 1916 or 3.2.16 on the maps and in the indexes, otherwise the text is basically set out like the original.

~ ~ ~ ~ ~ ~ ~ ~ ~

Transcriber's note

It has been a salutary task transcribing my father's diary, and something I have had in mind for a long time as I felt I owed it to his memory. He went through so much danger and horror for his family and his country. It is sad that so many of his compatriots failed to return, and remarkable that he survived. This is not the place to discuss the rights and wrongs of the Great War – however, it is amazing to realise that only some twenty years later he had the grief of seeing the same countries conquered and occupied by Nazi German forces during the Second World War. I remember as an eleven-year old the French capitulation in June 1940 and my father's sadness at the time. He was encouraged by the appointment of 84-year old Marshal Pétain ("he's a good man") as prime-minister and then head of state, but was appalled by his setting up the Vichy French government which collaborated with Hitler.

Edward Raymond Hepper was born on 19 July 1892 in Leeds. His parents were Edward Henry Hepper and Gertrude Emily Hepper (née Bedford). He joined his father's firm Hepper & Sons, Chartered Surveyors, Auctioneers and Estate Agents; volunteered for the West Yorkshire Regiment in December 1914 as Second Lieutenant; he was demobilised in January 1919 as Captain, and rejoined his firm. He married Ada Cecilia Heasman in 1924, who died in May 1963. On 10 June 1965 he married my god-mother Flora Muriel Steel Lacey. He died on 15 April 1970 in Leeds.

Although I have driven through the battlefield region several times and seen the monuments from afar, it was during a short tour organised by Remembrance Travel/British Legion in May 2008 that I had the privilege of going to the Arras area. We visited the British Memorials at Delville Wood,

Theipval (Monument to the Missing), Serre (Lancashire Fusiliers), Ulster Tower, and Contay War Cemetery near Amiens, as well as the two Canadian Memorials (Newfoundland & Vimy Ridge). Everywhere was green and beautiful without any clue as to the devastated landscape during the Great War.

While my father was still alive I remember him telling me how he compiled the diary. He said that his parents kept his letters which he used, together with his own notes for writing up the diary in neat form whenever he was at home on leave. Judging by the personal details, he must have kept daily notes from which he prepared the final copy.

I hope that historians and other researchers will find this transcription useful, and forgive any errors I have made. The text should now be much more accessible than on microfilm at the Imperial War Museum. I am grateful to the staff of the Museum for their help, and especially to Mr Tony Richards, Mr Roderick Suddaby and Mr Peter Hart. Thanks too, to my wife Helen for checking the text with me and Marielle Graham for checking the place-names, and to Dawn Robertson of Hayloft Publishing for taking it on.

~ ~ ~ ~ ~ ~ ~ ~ ~

Aspects of Captain E.Raymond Hepper army service shown in his Great War diary:

A pioneer of the interpretation of aerial photography
It is hard for us to realise that at the outbreak of the Great War aeroplanes were only a few years old and still quite primitive. Yet this was the first time that the enemy's lines could be spied upon and photographed from the air. True, balloons had often been used for that purpose, but they were more or less static, whereas aeroplanes could go where they wanted at various heights. Reports from reconnaisance flights by the Royal Flying Corps (RFC) were not immediately appreciated by Henry Wilson who rejected them, according to Robin Neillands (*The Old Contemptibles*, p. 119).

But aerial photography soon proved valuable, although it must have been difficult for the pilot to take photographs with a heavy plate glass camera which had to be manhandled in the open cockpit. Aerial photographs provided the troop commanders with valuable information about enemy emplacements that were out of sight from the ground. What was needed was to extract the relevant details and my father did this by tracing the prints and preparing hand-drawn maps containing information that was likely to be useful.

Father had received professional training as a chartered surveyor for the family firm of Hepper and Sons of Leeds. Evidently, this became known to his superiors who detailed him to prepare such plans. The diary entries about maps appear frequently, "Most of the time is spent in drawing maps,

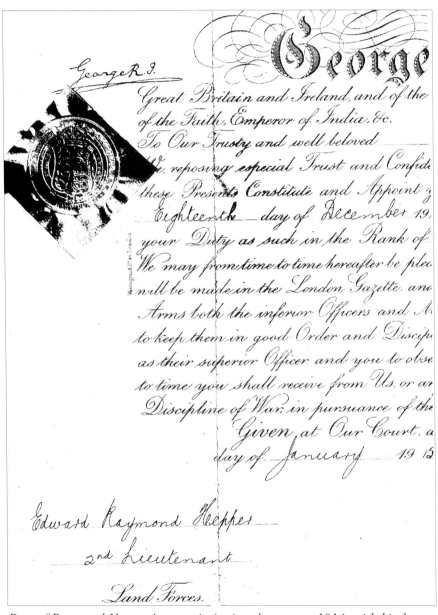

Part of Raymond Hepper's commissioning document, 1914, with kind permission of the National Archives.

James Bedford, when the Lord Mayor of Leeds, on the steps of Leeds Town Hall. He signed Raymond's enlistment papers in 1914.

entering aeroplane photographs" (25.10.16). A few days later he writes, "Busy as usual with air photos and reports," (2 and 4.11.16). "Very busy preparing large maps for handing over, also aeroplane photographs." "I am busy preparing maps of the front line," (7.3.17) and "I make another contour map," (19.3.17). He also had the task of plotting the old three-mile railway line leading to part of the Somme battlefield west of St Quentin. His plans for its renovation were well received by the Colonel, much to his elation (20 and 21.3.17). In Octber 1917, he applied, "for the Intelligence Corps as Branch Intelligence Officer attached to the Flying Corps for interpretation of air photographs."

A Naturalist on the Western Front

One may ask how anyone could be a naturalist during the horrors of the Great War. While transcribing my father's diary I came across frequent references to wildlife. I find this hardly surprising, however, knowing of his interest in plants and animals - a love of which he passed on to me in due course, and my work at Kew Herbarium.

On the battlefield in 1916-1919 he was in his early twenties and it was only a few years since he had founded the Field Club at his school, Wrekin College at Wellington in Shropshire. I recall him telling me that the Club's

West Yorkshire Regiment recruits and bands in training at Ilkley in 1915.

field trips were very popular with boys since in the strict school régime they were the only occasions when they were allowed outside the walls. The school magazine of 1910 gives a report of a lecture given by my father to the Club entitled '*British Wild Life*'. In it he pointed out what a great amount of pleasure can be obtained from nature study and he hoped his lecture would have the effect of awakening interest in the subject. He further said that, "one of the greatest lessons of nature was that of mercy," unaware of the merciless terrors that were imminent in his life. In December 1914 he volunteered for service as a 2nd Lieutenant in the West Yorkshire Regiment (later promoted to Captain). He trained at Ilkley during 1915 with no inkling that he was to spend most of the next three years being shot at in the muddy trenches of the Somme and Ypres battlefields.

In January 1916 he crossed the Channel to France and headed for the front line. On the night of 20 February he wrote in his diary that in spite of bursting 'Very' lights: "there is an owl which seems like the appeal of a lost soul." That owl would have been the familiar tawny, *Stix aluco*.

Then on 13 March he wrote: "The day is perfect, the birds are singing everywhere and if one did not hear the occasional burst of a Hun shell and our own artillery reply, he could sit down at the stagnant pools and dream that he was at home... bird, insect and fish life seem to take no notice of war. The other day after the bombardment a little lark mounted above no-man's-land singing his blythe song as if nothing had happened." Later, stuffed birds at Vandricourt Chateau museum which originally belonged to an Englishman, attract comment: "The chateau has been utterly destroyed and traces of stuffed birds, bits of furniture and bound copies of *Country Life* are strewn about the grounds" (11 April 1917).

Although my father was keen on watching birds and finding their nests, his first love was the collection and pressing of wild flowers that he made into dried specimens which formed his own herbarium of British flora. When in France he went to the Forest of Nieppe near Merville (23 March 1916) he noted that, "it is a beautiful typically French wood with long straight rides. Wood anemones [*Anemone nemorosa*] and oxlips [*Primula elatior*] carpet the ground." He evidently knew the distinction between primroses, cowslips and the much less common oxlip. Shortly afterwards (10 April) he was, "just off for a march. It is a glorious morning and the hedges are in blossom and full out," adding rather condescendingly, "Really, France looks quite pretty today." Two days later (25 April), "There is quite a good garden in this billet and we spend our time reading among the flowers." Then on 1 September he was admiring the Padré's begonias! The following September, on the 27th, on his way to Boulogne my father commented on, "the pretty River Somme where roses were still in the gardens which skirt the river and here and there the Somme widens and is filled with waving rushes," which also associated with yellow flags, *Iris pseudacorus* (21 March 1917).

As a naturalist he extended his observations to all wildlife. For example on 12 May 1916 he wrote: "I pay a visit to Hazebrouch one day. The country is beautiful and we are nestled at the foot of a wood and at night the air

In training at Ilkley: Raymond Hepper back row, sixth from right.

Above, Spruce Picea abies *and, below, Scots pine* Pinus sylvestris.

is so full of a perpetual hum of croaking bull frogs. It is like a dozen corncrakes in a singing competition." At that period corncrakes were still common in the cornfields of the Yorkshire Dales where they must have been well known to him.

On one of his long marches near Arras he asked, "Why do all French roads have an avenue of poplars?" and then answered the question himself. "I understand that Napoleon constructed the straight military roads and as the poplar was a favourite tree of his, the avenues were planted in consideration of him."

During a tour of duty in Belgium behind Ypres he stayed at army HQ based in a mansion, "situated in a park surrounded by a very wide belt of copper beeches such as I have never seen in my life before. It is like a scene from a theatre."

After the Armistice was signed on 11 November 1918 he had to march his Company, often in drenching rain, through eastern Belgium north of Luxemburg. Even so he wrote that, "The country is magnificent. The district is very hilly, being similar to Roseberry Topping and the Cleveland Hills in Yorkshire, and they are practically covered from top to foot with spruce and pines." (11.12.18)

Some days before (26.11.18), he had borrowed a bicycle to catch up the marching troops: "I ride on towards the Meuse, a few miles away. What a noble river! A suspension bridge is thrown across and at the other side the village of Yvoir nestles under the limestone cliffs through which the river flows. At the foot of the cliffs the trees are still retaining their autumn tints and contrast with the dark firs which interspace."

They crossed the frontier at Poteau into Germany as part of the Rhineland occupation force. A few days later, they made friends with the local gamekeeper in his lodge, and another facet of my father's countryside interests is revealed, "The house is a little chalet and hung inside with the usual trophies. This fellow is a fine strapping man, too old for the army and clad in Sherwood green with acorn epaulets to his typically military coat. On his head is a green homberg with the Imperial Eagle badge and at the side a blackcock's tail." Unfortunately it was snowing and game would be sheltering, the gamekeeper warned. However on 20 December 1918 they ventured out and, "in many places we come across the spore of wild boar [*Sus scrofa*] and roebuck [*Capreolus capreolus*] and in two cases that of a large stag, but our guide is correct and we see nothing."

Soon after the New Year 1919 while they were occupying Commern in the hills south of Cologne, he writes, "We have exciting hare hunts," this is the brown hare, *Lepus europaeus*. "The battalion forms a square of one company at each side of nearly a mile wide. At a given signal we close in and in doing so encircle a number of hares; on one occasion there were as many as sixteen but only three were caught. He who catches a hare is entitled to keep it. Everyone gets vastly excited and thoroughly enjoys the sport," which would hardly be acceptable nowadays.

Humour and culture amid death and destruction
I recall my father as a twentieth century Mr Pickwick, short and rotund with a ready wit and a twinkle in his eye. He was also a cultured man, knowledgeable about antiquities and stamps, as well as fine art and history. We would go on family outings with the Yorkshire Thoresby Society to see historic Roman villas, ancient churches and even to Civil War battlefields, and study coins together. Even in his war diary of his own battlefields where death and destruction were very real, his twinkle persisted.

For example, bathing was an essential treat to wash off the accumulated mud, he noted, "Had a delightful bath at Croix Barbée. Just fancy bathing under shell fire" (19.4.16). Worse, a few days later he, "expected every minute a crump would land on the bath-house… and I would have to run out with 'nothing on.' How awfully infradig." Another time the men had found baths in the brewery which caused him to comment, "There should be a good beer later, plenty of body." (8.2.16).

Being quite familiar with amateur dramatics in Leeds, he had up his sleeve certain party pieces which could be rolled out at army frivolities organised to keep the troops happy. On Christmas Day 1916 he states in his diary that at a 'French Mortar Battery concert' he gave a recitation, possibly in French. The following February at the village of Havernas behind the lines, during an organised concert attended by the local countess and family, he recited in English 'The Wedding Speeches,' whatever they were.

Un-rehearsed situational comedy in the most unlikely places amused him, too. When relieving another company it was necessary to squeeze along trenches, "and after a good deal of wriggling" to pass one another. Unfortunately while under shell-fire they met a fellow officer who was "extraordinarily fat" and found it difficult to pass along a communication trench only fifteen inches wide.

My father was more of a horseman than I had realised before reading his diary. He rode frequently but favoured a pony which was small and docile. "I go up the line on my pony. Have I introduced you to the 'Little'un'? A black mare of about 14 hands, with white star, shaggy mane and pretty tail, well fed and groomed, groggy forelegs and a quiet disposition, she has probably been a lady's pony at some time and I know that I am fairly safe while riding as she does not kick or bite, doesn't run away, doesn't exert herself. The 'Little'un' has only three speeds, slow – damn slow – and stop. She is, however, pleasanter than the one I had in England which always did want to go the way you didn't, and sometimes went, too," (27 February 1917).

Unfortunately, the Little 'un was taken away by the artillery, so he borrowed one from the mobile stable. He wrote that this, "horse I have borrowed from the mobile has just thrown me. As we were crossing a narrow ditch when he kicked out and over I went into the mud. When I looked back the horse was careering home and was eventually caught by Bell's groom about half a mile away," (21 November 1917).

His army cooks who kept stirring their soup while oblivious of enemy bombardments were always a source of comfort and fun. "I am intensely amused," he writes, "on reaching our embankment to find our fat old cook McDonald (of the 17th Royal Scots) sitting on his haunches, howling down curses on the Germans who made him leave his beautiful piece of roast mutton he was preparing for our dinner. 'Why did Ah no breeing it wi me, Sirs?' was his wail… 'As nice a piece as iver Ah did see.'" Father comments, "Poor old McDonald your meat is quite safe and after all what is the price of meat with the price of one's life?" (30.4.17)

In a different vein, Father was observant of beauty and history when he travelled behind the Lines. "The old town of Doullens," he writes, "set in a valley amid rolling hills calls for a stop and as the day is very hot, we spend an enjoyable hour." (31.8.16). Later that day he comments on the scenery, "The district around Lucheux and Sus St Leger is fine. The old village of Lucheux is situated on the side of a hill surrounded by beautiful woods and far up this the old chateau or castle looks out over the expanse of trees." Fine architecture is admired too, "What a lovely place Arras has been. Its narrow cobbled streets, its rows of little ancient and carved stone houses, one of which Robespierre was born in, and its Grand Place surrounded by staircase-gabled Spanish-Flemish arched buildings" (29.10.16).

Lieutenant Hepper, left, with fellow officers soon after completion of their training in 1915.

The Somme gets a very poor image in most accounts of the Great War, and stands for death and destruction with good reason. So it seems remarkable that Father could refer to the Somme as a "pretty river"(10.2.17). Near Péronne he exclaimed, "What a glorious part of the country this is! Undulating valley rolling up from the banks of the Somme with its beds of rushes and iris." (21.3.17).

All the same, the Somme battlefields were truly horrific, and yet a couple of days after an attack Father and colleagues were searching for strawberries to buy at the local chateau where he chatted to the resident's daughter (7.7.16). Yes, life goes on. Yet at the end of July 1916 he himself was in the thick of the battle, "Horror on horror… the barrage continues to fall all along the trench. God, this is awful. Shall we ever get out alive?" That day's entry in his Diary concluded, "It is useless putting into writing the sights I have seen today for they will ever be in my mind as a momento of July 30."

In January 1919 my father was demobilised in Shropshire and returned to resume his work as a Chartered Surveyor and Auctioneer with Hepper and Sons at Hepper House in East Parade, Leeds. He wrote on the final page of his diary, "I draw a curtain over times in which there have been many glimpses of sunshine thro' the thunder clouds and I look forward to the happiness of Peace." How sad that some twenty years later he was to witness Nazi forces sweeping across the former Western Front, this time resulting in the capitulation of the France he had grown to love. He had actually returned there for his honeymoon in 1924.

Summary of Diary

See Maps 1-8: (pages 57-63) where the date is the first time the place is mentioned in the diary. The spelling is usually as written but often modified on later published maps. A few extra place-names are added to maps in order to help with locations.

Frame numbers: As the printed text is based on microfilm of the manuscript at the Imperial War Museum, the selection of frame numbers entered here provides an approximate guide for subsequent users. However, note that they may vary according to how the film is fed into the reader.

1916
31 January	Southampton for Channel crossing	Frame 3

ARRIVAL IN FRANCE
heading for the Somme battlefield trenches

1916
1,2 February	Le Havre/Harfleur	Frame 4
3	Rouen, Buchy	
4	Boulogne, Calais, Campagne (E of St Omer)	Frame 5
7	Baudringhem, Racquinhem, Belle Croix, Wardrecques, Arques	
9	Boeseghe	
13	Oise	Frame 8
18	Forêt de Nieppe, St Vincent, Havers-Kerque, Merville	
19	Le Sart, Merville	
20	Pont du Hene, La Gorgue	Frame 10
22	Pont du Hene, Laventie	Frame 15
24	La Gorgue, Merville	
27	La Flingue, Pont du Hene, Riez Bailleul, La Gorgue, Merville	
28	La Vena, Merville	
29	River Lys, Merville	

1916

2 March	La Gorgue	Frame 16
6	L'Epinette	Frame 17
7	Pont du Hene, La Gorgue	
10	Neuve Chapelle, Chapigny Farm	
12	Annéquin	Frame 20
13	Epinette Farm	
14	Paradis near Merville, Loos	
16	Pacault, Calonne	
19	Le Sart, Béthune, Beuvry, Annequin, Cinchy, Auchy, La Bassée, Merville, Calonne	Frame 21
23	Les Lauriers, Forêt de Nieppe, Champ de Tir	
24	Merville Station, Armentieres	Frame 22
25	Estaires, Bac St Maur	
26	Neuf-Berquin	Frame 23
3 April	Sailly, Estaires, Neuf-Berquin	
5	La Gorgue, Estaires	
6	Estaires	Frame 27
8	Sailly	
11	Estaires, Laventie	
15	Laventie	

Ilkley Railway Station, 1915, from where the trained recruits headed for the trenches in France.

1916		
16	Croix Barbée	
19	Croix Barbée	Frame 31
23	Neuve Chapelle	
28	Les Lobes, Croix Barbée	Frame 33
29	Béthune	
3 May	Calonne, Paradis	
5	Lestrem	
6	Richebourg, Rue du Bois	
11	Richebourg, Neuve Chapelle	Frame 34
12	Steenbecque, Hazebrouck	
22	Croix Marmeuse	Frame 37
23-26	Nieppe Forest Range	
27	Festubert	
28	Festubert	
30	Festubert	
1 June	Le Touret	Frame 39
12	Croix Marmeuse	
16	Hingette (? Hinges), Béthune	
19	Rue d'Aire, Arras	Frame 40
	Arras	Frame 41

TO THE SOMME BATTLEFIELD,

1916		
29 June	Gonnehem, Le Souich near Doullens	
1 July	Le Souich	Frame 45
5	Le Souich, Bois de Warremont, Thiepval, Ovillers, Serre	
7	Anthee	
9	Bresle, R. Somme crossed	Frame 46
	Bois Celestine	
	Billone Wood	
12	Carnoy valley, Talus Bois, G(u)illemont, Montauban Wood, Delville Wood, Ginchy, Albert, Hardecourt, South Montauban Trench	
22 onwards	Bernafay, Bernafay Wood, Waterlot Farm	Frame 51

1916
29	Caftet, Caftet Wood, Briquetesil, Maricourt, South Bernafay Trench, Dublin Trench, Casement Trench, Maltzhorn Ridge	
30	Bernafet Trench, G(u)illemont	Frame 53
31	Caftet Wood	
1 August	Sandpit Valley	Frame 55
2	Sandpit Valley, Poziéres, Méaulte	
3?	Morlancourt	
11	Somme battle area, Hauguest near Picguiny, Morlancourt	
16	Sandpit Valley	Frame 56
18	Contour Wood, Caftet Wood, Billone Wood, Arrowhead Copse, Maltzhorn Trench	
23	Silesia Trench	
24	Champagne Trench, Maltzhorn Valley, Mametz, Lonely Trench	
25	Leuza Wood, Le Forest, Combles	
27	Talus Boise, Maltzhorn Ravine, Casement Trench, Happy Valley	Frame 58
28	Happy Valley, Bois Celestines	
29	Albert Road, Amiens to Autheux, Canaples, Bernaville	Frame 66
31	Doullens, Lucheux, Sus St Leger	
2 September	Hauteville, Arras	
3	Avesnes-le-Comte	
5	Duisans	Frame 67
7	Avesnes-le-Comte	
9	Arras	
10	St Nicholas Arras, Sunday Avenue	
11	(Thelus, Farbus/Farber, Willerval, Mondry)	Frame 69
12	Kiek Crater	
16	Roclincourt, Wednesday Avenue	
18	Roclincourt, Arras	Frame 71
20	Arras	
22	King & Kite Craters, Laurence Avenue	
26	Sunday Avenue, Arras, Duisans, Aubigny, Boulogne (Villiards)	

1916
LEAVE IN LEEDS, 27 September to 7 October 1916

RETURN TO ARRAS and SOMME BATTLEFIELD TRENCHES

1916

8 October	Boulogne (Louvre Hotel)	Frame 73
9	Duisans	
12	Katie Crater	
29	Arras, Pont du Jour, Ecurie, Roclincourt	Frame 75
2-3 November	Victoria Street, Kent & Katie Craters	Frame 81
13	Gridiron line, Pope's Nose	Frame 84
25-26	King Crater	
3 December	Haute-Avesnes, Foufflin [Ricaud], St Pol	Frame 91
7-22	[sniper class]	
19	Arras	
30	Liguy Schloss	Frame 94

LEAVE IN LEEDS, 8-18 January 1917

RETURN TO SOMME BATTLEFIELD, January 1917

1917

19 January	Return to France	
6 February	Fortel	Frame 95
7	Fortel, Rebreuve Chateau, Outrebois, Doullens	
8	Havernas, Vignacourt, Yzeux, Picquiney	
10	Somme	
17	Vignacourt (for photo)	

MOVE TO FRENCH SECTOR NEAR ROSIERES, February 1917

19 February	Marcelcave	Frame 103
22	Caix	
24	Caix, Champs des Ballons	
26	Rosières	
28	Chateau of Chaulnes, Bois Broussig, Rosthnais	
3 March	Bois Frederic	Frame 106
6-14	Rosières	
15	Caix, Arras, Roye, [Dixmude,] Hindenburg Line	
17	Rosières, Roye, Chaulnes Chateau	

1917

18	Omiécourt, Hallincourt, Manicourt	Frame 107
20	Hallu-Chilly, Chaulnes-Omiécourt	
21	Hallu, Chilly, Maucourt, Curchy,	
	Puisieux/Puzeaux, Omiécourt, Punchy,	
	Bois de Hallu, Marchlepot, Epanancourt,	
	River Somme, St Christ, Pargny,	
	Ennemain, Falvy, Athies, Prusle,	
	Flamicourt, Péronne, Vermand,	
	Monchy-Lagache, Cartigny Farm	

10 April	Vermand, Omignon stream, St Christ	Frame 113
11	Omignon, Bellicourt, Hallie Wood,	
	Vandricourt Chateau, St Quentin canal,	
	Hindenburg line, Bellenglise,	
	Magny-la-Fosse, Etricourt, Tronquoy	
13	Holnon	
14	Maissemy, Nauroy, Magny-la-Fosse	
16	St Helene salient	
23	Cuvigny farm, Tertry, Caulaincourt	
30 April to	Vermand, Masteville cutting, R. Omignon, Falvy,	
12 May	Gricourt, Fayet, Les Trois Sauvages, Cepy	

19 May	Estrées-Péronne	Frame 126
21	Sorrel le Grand, Bussu cross-roads	
23	Villers-Guislain, Raileau Mill	
24	Villers-Guislain	
29	Villers-Guislain, Hindenberg Line, La Terriere,	
	Lateau Wood, les Rues des Vignes,	
	Chenaux Wood, Honnecourt	

2 June	Templeux la Fosse, Henne woods, Aizecourt	
3 June-22 July	Epehy & Lempire, Villers-Guislain	Frame 131

28 July	Longavesnes	

6 August	G(u)illemont Farm	Frame 144
11	G(u)illemont Farm	
	G(u)illemont Farm, Lempire, Amiens,	
	Soyecourt, Roisel, Ronssoy,	

1917

1 September	Aizecourt	Frame 153
6	Epehy	
8	Villers-Guislain, Péronne	
13	Birdcage	
16	Aizecourt	
23	Amiens	
26	Péronne, Amiens	
27	Amiens, Boulogne, Abbéville	

LEAVE IN LEEDS, 28 September to 7 October 1917

RETURN TO FRANCE, October 1917

8 October	Boulogne	
9	Mont St Eloi, Agnez-lés-Duisans, Duisans, Arras, Ypres	
11-13	Dainville	
14	Arneke near Cassel, Rudbroreck/Rubrouck	
15	Cassel, St Omer, Dunkerque, St Sylvestre Capell	
16	Arneke, Berques, Proven	Frame 166
17	De Wippe Cabaret (Belgium), Henley Wood	
18 October	Elverdinghe, Boesinghe, Decauville railway, Langemarck, Forest of Houethulst/Houthulst, Fourck Farm, Fourch Farm, Wood 15, Boesinghe cross-roads	
20	Carency p. de C., Zoomer Bloom, De Wippe Cabaret-Elverdinghe	
27	Proven, Boesinghe, Poona Camp,	
30	De Wippe Cabaret (Beuson's Farm)	
4 November	Proven, Poperinghe	
8	Pitt Camp, Proven, Porchester Camp, Elverdinghe, Zoomer Bloom	
26	Brielen	Frame 169
1 December	Godewaersvelde, Thieushouk	
2	Merville, Le Sart	
3	L'Eclemée (near Chocgues)	
4	Barlin	
5	Acq, Mont St Eloi	
22	Mory, Bullencourt, Ecwist, Station Redoubt	Frame 174

1918

1 January	Boisleux, Warecourt, Héninel, Hindenberg Line, Cherisey, La Fontaine-les-Croisilles, Monchy-les-Preux, Arras-Cambrai, Vis-en-Artois	Frame 181

INTELLIGENCE TRAINING COURSE IN ENGLAND,
January to October 1918

RETURN TO FRANCE to Cambrai,
October 1918 and Armistice 11 November 1918

16 October	Boulogne, St Martius Camp, Cambrai, Carnières, Bévillers, Solesmes	Frame 191

3 November	Solesmes	
4	Escarmain	
5	Ruesnes, Le Quesnoy, Orsinval	
6	Petit Marais, Gommegnies, Forêt de Mormal, Le Cheval Blanc	
7	Obies, Tayompret	Frame 220
8	Mecquignies, Cheneau Loup [=Quene-au-Leu], Bois Delahaye	
9	Mecquignies, Maubeuge	
10	Sous le Bois (Maubeuge), (Mons)	Frame 224
11	Armistice: hostilities cease	
15	Maubeuge	

MARCH THROUGH SOUTH EASTERN BELGIUM heading for occupation of GERMANY south of Cologne,
November 1918 to January 1919

16	Maubeuge, Ferrière-la-Grand	
18	Bousignus, Beaumont	
19	Gozée, Thouin/Thuin	
20	Gozée, Thouin/Thuin	
24	Mettet	Frame 229
25	Warnant, R. Meuse	
26	R. Meuse, Yvoir, Spontin, Soret	Frame 232
27	Ciney, Chapois, (Solesmes)	

1918

2 December	Leignon	Frame 236
10	Maffe	
11	River l'Ourthe, Hamoir	
12	Ernonheid	Frame 238
	Basse-Bouloque/Bodeux?	
14	Les Trois-Ponts, Grand Halleux, Vielsalm	
16	Poteau (German frontier), Recht, Born	
17	Honningen/Hunningen	Frame 241
20	Malmédy	
21	Hellenthal	
24	Kommern/Commern, Euskirchen (Ramur),	
26	Kommern/Commern	

1919

1 January	Kommern/Commern	
4	Cologne, Micherincht, R. Rhine	
1919		
5	Cologne, Kommern/Commern	Frame 245
6-16	Bonn, Rhine, Düren, Aix la Chapelle, Liège, Namur, Charleroi, Tournai, Lille, Dunkirk	Frame 250

Demobilised in Prees Heath, Shropshire

Captain E. Raymond Hepper's Great War Diary, 1916-1919

HEAVENS! How time flies. We have been in training thirteen months and now it is time to put to test all we have learnt.

Southampton

31 January 1916

The Durhams are still waiting in the station - poor beggars. They left **Perham Down** at 4.30 this morning and we left at 3.00 this afternoon and we shall be 'over the water' before them.

The *Mauritania* is in harbour - a fine boat painted grey and used as a Hospital Ship. Our boat is the *Duchess of Argyll* used originally as a Clyde pleasure steamer - she has a good speed. No "tin fishes" [torpedoes] seen.

ARRIVAL IN FRANCE, heading for trenches east of Merville

1 February 1916

Arrived at **Harfleur** or rather at **Havre** at 1am. Had to wait until light to disembark. Disgusting now to find that we are to walk six miles to camp at **Harfleur** of Shakespeare fame. Phew! What packs, what on earth made me bring so much stuff?

Worse still; **Harfleur** reached but find we are not expected; have to wait until tents arrive. Tried to post a letter but forgot it had to have the censor's stamp.

Awfully funny, I have just met **Colonel Pollard** who raised the Regiment; he recognised me quite a long way off - I was awfully bucked. We went onto the parade ground together and the men sent up a good old cheer. **Colonel Atkinson** couldn't make out what was happening as the men were on parade ready to move off. Great breach of discipline. Speech by Colonel. We then fix brown bell tents. Have arranged to mess with the Guards and meet their **Chaplain Canon Hannay** of Great George at Birmingham.

2 February 1916

Generally hang round the parade ground and do nothing. **Huffam** and I got to **Havre** and thoroughly enjoy it. It is a peculiar place but the shops are useful.

The battalion has just moved off from **Harfleur** to **Havre** station. It is now 9.15pm. **Huffam, Redman** and myself with 124 men are the rear party and are moving in the morning. I think we have "the crow" over the rest of the battalion, we shall have a good sleep in our valises.

3 February 1916

Still dark - just going to move off. A stroke of luck - I am detailed for the Ration Party and the motor lorry is just leaving - thus I miss a six-mile march in full kit.

Have drawn rations at Gare des Marchandises and I meet the company as it marches into the station. We arrange ourselves in cattle trucks marked Hommes et Chevaux 8. The men collect straw and hay from the platform and make good beds in the trucks. The Durhams are on the train but had not thought of collecting this and we have none to spare.

As usual we have <u>only</u> to wait three hours before the train condescends to move. 11.59 at last we are off. We understand that the journey will last two days - lucky there are only three of us in our carriage. Very interesting journey, but not pretty. We pass **Rouen** and stop at **Buchy**. Delightful ladies are serving at a stall on the platform. It is fine to see an English woman's face again even though we have only been over the water a couple of days. Have coffee and cognac for the first time and now it won't be the last. Sleep the rest of the way and woke up at **St Omer** and find it is six o'clock on – [4 Feb.]

4 February 1916

We search the station for water, boil the dixies and hear more disconcerting news. We have been brought to the wrong station and must march seven miles. The men are delighted? We meet our guide, a delightful fellow who can say a few words in English and is labelled Interpreter. We learn that we have passed through **Calais** and **Boulogne** during our sleep, we can at any rate say we have been there.

We join the Battalion at **Campagne** arriving there at 1pm and met by **Cohen** who conducts us to our billets. Jolly good ones too. It has been decided that we should sleep in the farmhouse which constitutes Company Headquarters, bedroom and living rooms. **Huffam** now wants this to himself. **Cohen, Cross** and myself find an achievable little cottage with two bedrooms, a living room and kitchen. Our three servants live in the kitchen and are delighted with the house. Of course if your servant is pleased with the place then it is quite alright; all three get on very well together and none of us want to do any more work for the rest of our lives. The dear old lady, **Madame Loudries,** retires to her room and leaves us in peace.

Cheers, I haven't forgotten what little French I knew and can get along quite well.

5 February 1916

Getting settled into billets. An aeroplane is flying overhead - they're shelling it. **Huffam** is lecturing us but we all run out and see the [plane] which is most exciting. Each man has written about four letters on the subject, i.e. for my platoon at least 240 letters, so I am rather fed up with it as we censor the letters of our platoon. One can get too much of a good thing.

A sample page from the diary, covering part of 24, 25 and 26 February 1916.

6 February 1916
I am Orderly Officer. Nothing doing.

7 February, 1916
Battalion route march to **Baudringhem, Racquinhem, Belle Croix** and **Wardrecques.** 5.30pm just off to **Arques** for provisions.

8 February 1916
I instruct the snipers on the canal bank during the morning, the remainder of the men are bathing in the brewery. There should be a good beer later, plenty of body. **Huffam** goes to the trenches.

9 February 1916
Beastly hard luck, we have to leave our famous cottage and trek to **Boeseghem.** On the road, word is passed down that **Sir Douglas Haig** is reviewing us. He is a fine man. Later we are again reviewed, this time by **Prince Arthur of Connaught;** gave a good salute and got a "good morning" from him.

10 February 1916
Settled down in billets which are rather far from one another. Three of us, **Cohen, Cross** and self are 'digging' in a little cottage. It is a squash and we decide that **Cross** shall sleep at another farm and **Cohen** and I remain where we are. However, we mess with **Cross.**

11 February 1916
We are standing in three inches of water waiting for **Lord Kitchener.** Two hours later - still waiting. Two hours later still - **Lord Kitchener** arrives, receives the salute, walks along the front of each Battalion and departs. We are soaked through and several men have fainted. Amused how quickly staff chauffeurs drive cars backwards.

12 February 1916
Recovering from awaiting of **Lord Kitchener.** Washing clothes. C.O. lectures in afternoon.

13 February 1916
Rainy day. Paraded for church parade and found there wasn't one. Just have been down to **Oise** shopping. Visited the Cathedral of St Pierre and were not particularly entranced with it as it is decorated inside with crude colours from top to foot. The choir, as most French choirs do, sounded very

hoarse. Bought *La Vie Parisienne* for **Cross.** Believe he rather likes it - naughty man.

14 February 1916
Instruct in scouting and sniping. The guns can be heard in the distance. There was a big strafe on Saturday night.

15 February 1916
Again parade with scouts and snipers. All officers attend a lecture at **Aire** by **General Hakin**, our Corps Commander; it is very interesting and there is comic business with late comers.

16 February 1916
Delivered various lectures to scouts; **Sergt. Hayton** also lectured. Fiddled about generally in the afternoon.

17 February 1916
Again parading with snipers and show them the uses of the telescope and maps. Clean up billets in the afternoon preparatory to moving.

18 February 1916
We line up at Headquarters at about 8 o'clock to march to our new quarters at **Merville.** We are having a heavy march and our shoulders ache with our equipment. **Butler** in my platoon is making everyone laugh at his remarks - and he calls Estaminets - Testaments. Passing **Forêt de Nieppe**. A magnificent road runs through the forest to **Havers-Kerque** and **St Vincent**.

We arrive at **Merville** and trail through the town, lose ourselves as usual and trail back again to meet **Rose**. Everyone frightfully annoyed. Managed to obtain quite a nice billet on the Rue de Béthune. 6.30 Rain coming down in torrents but **Cohen, Redman** and I brave the elements in order to have a good feed in **Merville**. I always thought that Hotel de Ville meant Town Hall but we also find that they provide an excellent dinner there. We can see the "Very Lights" from here**.**

19 February 1916
We have been put into the wrong billets and as we generally manage either to do this or lose our way we are not surprised. We therefore transfer our kit to **Le Sart** at the other side of **Merville,** and find that the billeting area allotted to us could take only 50 men. Much strafing and billet finding. We received orders last Friday to proceed to the trenches for instruction.

20 February 1916

Y and X Companies are to go straight into the trenches from here and I am afraid there is much grumbling. However, we parade at 10am and march to **La Gorgue**. Here a meal is provided for the men in the "Follies" Concert Hall and the canteen is going all hands to the pump. **Cohen, Crawford** and a number of officers flock to an estaminent [bar] and have a good " tuck in." Slow march to **Pont du Hene.** We pass a 4.7 gun on the road and a number of battered horses. At **Pont du Hene** cross-roads, we meet the guides of the 9th Welsh Fusiliers and proceed on a long slow march to the trenches. It hardly seems like war, occasionally there is the rattle of a machine gun, a few rifle shots and that is all - no not all - for Very lights are continually going up in their beautiful parabola, bursting at their highest point and flooding No Man's Land with light so that the stakes on which our wire is suspended appear at first like a long line of enemy attackers. Above this is heard the call of an owl which seems like the appeal of a lost soul. The communication trench is safely negotiated, a difficult task in the dark as one slip off the narrow track or duck board into the water beneath and wet feet are the cheerful result.

It is really difficult to put into words the first night [in the trenches], everything seems muddled. I remember finding a comfortable dugout on the left of the centre company but I spent most of the time walking round. I take my turn of watch with the others.

The tawny owl, Stix aluco.

21 February 1916

"Stand to" (at break of day). Rifle fire and bursts of machine gun fire rend the air but as yet we have had no shells over. The men seem to be taking it very well, though naturally there is a tendency to keep too much under cover.

Most of the day is being spent in inspection of the various trench methods which will be useful to us when we take a bit of line over on our own.

I have just met the scout officer and pump him for a few tips, he tells me that he is going out tonight and if I like to go with him I may do so. I naturally jump at the chance though I feel a bit queer.

11.30 just going out on patrol, my face is blackened with burnt cork to make it less visible. We i.e. seven, all look like Indians, in fact **Butler** in my platoon was frightfully scared as he said he didn't know that wild Indians were in the trench with him. Over the parapet into No-Man's-Land, just walking then crawling, crawling and apparently getting nowhere. We have finally arrived at a ditch not far from the German trench. A Very light is going up and it seems as if we have been spotted as a machine gun is traversing, not the parapet but the very ground around us. The patrol has now split into three, two to work along the ditch, and two in No-Man's-Land, and two along the ditch in front of our wire. I am with a corporal. Curse that machine gun - our very hair stands on end and we can hear or feel the bullets whistling round and so hastily decide that 'discretion is the better part of valour' and return.

In crossing the ditch I fall up to my neck but manage to swim out; it has apparently been an old trench. I then scramble through the wire occasionally sticking in the wire slip knots and gooseberries. 1.0am safe back but very wet. There is nowhere to dry clothes and I am, generally, fed up.

22 February 1916

Cohen is calling at my dugout and laughing at my plight, beastly fellow; hope he does the same sometime. Still wet, my things will not dry although I am practically sitting on a brazier. Hate war. We are being relieved tonight and shan't I just revel in being in a bed. We are trailing up the communication trench on our way to billets at **Pont du Hene**. The men are cleaning up this morning.

2.30pm Am detailed to take a party to the Boot Stores at **Laventie.** Men are cleaning up this morning

24 February, 1916

Getting ready for relief of trenches tonight. We have now relieved the Wilts and have gone in with the 10th Worcesters who came from **La Gorgue** tonight; the Welsh have gone back to **Merville**. Our new instructor seems to be a very nice fellow and better to get on with than the Welsh; we are in the right company.

We have been round the sentries and found 'all correct.' It has been snowing so we shall not send any more patrols out.

25 February 1916

The night has passed satisfactorily, in fact during the whole of today one would hardly think there was a war on; or perhaps the Hun knew we were in for instruction and wanted to let us down lightly.

26 February 1916
I have seen nothing of **Huffam** and **Cohen** today as they are in posts about a thousand yards behind the front line and they do not come down to the firing line. The Brigadier has been down and I have just shown him round the line.

27 February 1916
Spend a comfortable night in a barn at **La Flingue** cross-roads. It is dreadfully cold getting into one's valise. I am betimes. Our instruction has ceased and we are going back shortly. I join the company at **Pont du Hene** about 10 o'clock and we arrive at **Riez Bailleul** at 10.30 where the Colonel joins us and we march via **La Gorgue** to **Merville**.

Westcott finds his brother is at Flying School, went to **La Gorgue**.

The men are cheerfully grumpy as they have to carry such a heavy load - sheepskins, Macintosh sheets, etc.

2.30 we are back in the old billets at **Le Sart** and **Cohen** and I mess together. We have taken one of **Mason's** billets as ours, will not be fit to use as they are threshing beans. We do not expect **Mason** until tomorrow or the next day as they have to do another twelve hours in the trenches.

I have just heard that **Cohen** has been justly punished for laughing at me a few days ago for he has also fallen into a ditch on the night we were relieved. It is not a pleasant feeling.

28 February 1916
I am detailed to take a party to bathe at **La Vena.** The baths are worked on the geyser principle, undress in our room, rush into a hot spray, rush back into a cold room and out again, and all before you can say "kill". We had three miles to get there but the men say it was worth it.

I have returned and isn't it annoying, **Mason** has just arrived and claims his billet. My men are being put out into the road but fortunately the bean threshing is now finished and I can get back to my old billet.

Cohen and I have a "buster" in the town of **Merville**.

29 February 1916
I am afraid it wasn't much good washing yesterday as my men are cleaning out a coal barge this morning on the **River Lys.** It is a beautiful day and there are many air flights - a German aeroplane being brought down south of **Merville.** C.O's general talk.

British troops leaping across a trench, 1916.

1 March 1916

Cohen changes billets for the third time. We do nothing of note during the morning. The afternoon is given up to path laying. I believe if everything else fails we shall be [able] to turn our hands to path laying; we seem to do a bit of everything in the army. We have just got the path beautifully made when a note arrives from the orderly room informing us that we move tomorrow. Oh! Luckless path we shan't be able to use you after all.

2 March 1916

We move to **La Gorgue** and find a delightful billet in a large house. There is a washing bowl, and other toilet ware, a large mirror and wardrobe, things we have hardly seen before in our travels. The men are not well housed and the narrow, paved streets smell horribly.

3 March 1916

Black Friday, or so we call it. The company paraded under **Captain Huffam, Redman** and **Westcott** and went to the firing line in carts, as far as I can make out they have been cleaning out trenches. Most of the men get stuck in the mud and arrive back at 6pm. What grumbling and ?!!!

I have not had much to do today. The Col. wants all officers to attend a concert of the Divisional Follies. The show is rather a flop as only three officers and six rows of men are present.

4 March 1916

We are trying to dry the men's clothes which were saturated when on fatigue yesterday. I am detailed to go on the Corps Baths and shall have one myself.

5 March 1916

We attend Church Parade conducted by a Chaplain Major. The service is simple and thoroughly enjoyed by the men on the whole.

6 March 1916

I am on my way to a 'Flammenwerfer' [flamethrower] lecture at **L'Epinette,** I expect it will be fairly dry. Two hours later - Heavens! There is no lecture here. **Welches,** who is on a working party, informs me that there is another **L'Epinette** about 7 miles away, I believe I have put my foot in it this time. Yes I have, it is the other **Epinette.** My mistake is quite easily done as our other fatigue party people have been going to the former for the last two days. Fortunately, the lecture, I am told, only lasted ten minutes so we didn't miss much.

7 March 1916

We are today going to take a battalion line of our own. The morning is spent messing around getting billets cleaned up and the parade is ordered for four o'clock; we are decidedly more cheerful than those in Bainsfather's famous picture of 'Taking over the Trenches for the 200th Time'.

The realities of war - British troops burying dead colleagues in the war-blasted landscape of northern France, 1916.

Slow march to **Pont du Hene,** finally the trenches are relieved, bombers told off, sentries placed - exit Warwicks. Later when we hear from the Warwicks that it was the quickest relief they have ever had. They had ordered dinner at **La Gorgue** for twelve but thought they wouldn't get back until much later; as it was they were in **La Gorgue** at 10.0 and dinner was not ready. Not at all bad for our first relief, was it? **Crawford** went out on patrol.

8 March 1916

Marshall isn't up the line this tour, so I have taken over the snipers. Most of the morning I am spending in putting the snipers in their posts, pointing out their map readings and so on.

At 11.25 our 9.2 howitzers heavily shell the enemy's front line and isn't the mud flying, duckboards, rifles and probably people, appearing to go sky high. The Boshe retaliates but does practically no damage with the exception of blowing up a traverse of 9 Platoon's which they will have to build up again. There is very little happening during the afternoon.

9 March 1916

11.00 The field guns are wire cutting and shrapnel is just skimming our heads and bursting in front of the enemy's wire which is very thick at this point. In consequence of this wire cutting, our men i.e. X Company, have to keep down under the parados to prevent accident by stray bullets or prematures. I am observing with **Hamilton** through my telescopic periscope which the Battalion presented me with. Poor old **Styche** has just received some premature in the neck. He must have been walking behind the parados. He is dead.

The strafe is over and one of the artillery observers happens to be **Young** of Headingley. I did not know him but he has often seen me at St Chad's [Church, Far Headingley]. It is funny how one meets people in the trenches. This reminds me of another instance, one of the men has … [obscure] **R. Hitchin** of 1/7th W. Yorks is buried behind the parados of the front line.

10 March 1916

Today one of the heaviest bombardments I have seen has taken place. Fortunately it was against the German line not our own, which makes all the difference. 9.2 hows [howitzers] have been in action and on the left the D.87 (Field Guns) are still wire cutting. Away on our right is an intense shrapnel duel between our artillery and the German artillery in the vicinity of **Neuve Chapelle**. It was a really fine sight though some poor beggers must have got it in the neck. The Germans retaliated for our part of the strafe upon **Chapigny Farm** which is about a hundred yards behind the line and is used as an artillery O.P. [Observation Post].

We are all sitting round our dugout at 1 o'clock after the strafe every minute expecting something unpleasant in the way of trench mortars from the Hun, when in strolls one of our own artillery observers. "Good morning all. Can you let me have a ration biscuit or something to chew as mine have been blown up in the Farm." That was all, quite simple. What really had happened was this - three or four high explosive shells had burst right in the farm, where they were observing, throwing the officers around in all directions but luckily wounding no one. The boy's hand was trembling like an aspen, yet there was no complaint or no bragging. This thing goes on day after day all down the line. Surely the nation, when the war is over, will have some wonderful stories in her annals.

11 March 1916
We are coming out today; after all the four days of tour has gone fairly quickly though the second seemed endless.

I am handing over to the sniping officer of the Durhams and showing him the various danger spots and so on. We are just ambling along the parade trench when up above we hear a whistling sound, weeoo, weeoo, weeoo quite slowly at first then faster and we knew that it was a rifle grenade coming over, we bolt into a corner and bang our heads together. The grenade bursts harmlessly a few yards away. The men roar with laughter as we rub our poor bruised heads. I hate trench mortars and rifle grenades as they fall plumb on having reached the highest point in the air and thus if the range is correctly judged they will fall directly into the trench, whereas a shell, even a howitzer, has a wider curve and one can consequently get a little more protection.

One hour later. I am out before the rest of the battalion, what luck. **Crawford** has gone to arrange our billets. I meet him and we wait for the arrival of the company. The men have arrived and are very fatigued.

12 March 1916
Cohen and I get up very late. We were awakened at 7.30 by terrific bombardment, we wonder what it is and drop off to sleep again.

We find that the heavy firing this morning was retaliation for the hostile blowing up of a mine. A platoon of forty Highland Light Infantry were holding the **Duck's Bill**, a long lap protruding into No-Man's-Land. This had been mined by the Boche and blown up together with the forty HLI [Highland Light Infantry]. A counter attack is made to hold the outer lip of the crater formed by the explosion. This is successful and the officer in charge is the first in the Division to win the MC [Military Cross].

13 March 1916

I am on fatigue under shellfire at **Epinette Farm**. The men are carrying duck boards and wheeling stakes to the support line where a new work is proceeding. The day is perfect, the birds singing everywhere and if one did not hear the occasional burst of a Hun shell and our own artillery in reply, he could sit down by the stagnant pools and dream that he was at home. Bird, insect and fish life seem to take no notice of the war. The other day after the bombardment, a little lark mounted above No-Man's-Land singing his blithe song as if nothing had happened.*

The sky lark, Alauda arvensis, *is marvelled at in the diary entry as the bird sang its song above No-Man's-Land as if nothing had happened.*

14 March 1916

We have just had a few hours in **Paradis** near **Merville**. We reached here by companies and it was I believe the hottest day we have had in France. I think the village is the most English we have yet come across. I am lying upon the bank of one of the rear defences looking out over the flat ploughed fields to the distant hills beyond **Loos.**

We have an excellent mess room and my platoon is billeted in the same farm.

---

* This species used to be common in England as well as France, but its numbers are now greatly reduced owing to changes in land use.

15 March 1916

Battalion orderly officer, duties not arduous, glorious day.

16 March 1916

The battalion parades for a march to **Pacault** and **Calonne.** We have a supposed gas attack en route. Helmets are adjusted in record time.

17 March 1916

Nothing doing but the Battalion has been on manoeuvres.

18 March, 1916

We really have a complete rest these last few days. We are now drawing our steel helmets. (See colour photograph page 123).

19 March 1916

Another eventful day. The Battalion moves to **Le Sart** but I do not accompany it. **Huffam, Gill, Mason, Bell**, the Major and the CO, not omitting **Fricker** and myself journey on a motor bus to the trenches via **Béthune**.

Béthune is I believe the largest town I have been to in France. The picturesque boulevards, not yet out [i.e. trees in flower], run in all directions and the church and quaint belfry, evidently very ancient, stand out conspicuously.

Our journey continues past **Beuvry** to **Annéquin** and then after an interesting but shaky time we alight. Half an hour later – I am detailed to go round the trenches with the generals and the sniping officers to see their location and condition as we may have to take them over. Desolation everywhere; the ruined village of **Guinchy** behind our line and the battered town of **Auchy** behind the German Line, and further beyond is **La Bassée**. In the distance against the sky-line stands the **Loos** bridge.

It was here by the canal that **Michael O'Leary** won the VC. About eleven or twelve gaunt brick-stacks, battered and out of shape, stand half in our lines and half in theirs, and we play hide and seek with the Hun.

8.30 we are back at **Le Sart, Merville,** after the bumpy journey home. The Royal Scots are billeted at **Calonne** and we have had to go back via that place. It would have been much better to have walked from the cross-roads only **Mason** put his foot down and everyone acquiesced.

20 March 1916

All the company is billeted in one farm and we i.e. **Cohen** and I, are in a room in a small cottage about two hundred yards away. The people are charming and give one a delightful welcome. The father is an old French

Artillery man and we have a discussion on Patris, **Cohen** being chiefly the spokesman for the two. The Company is doing little work today. We dine at the Hotel de Ville.

21 March 1916

Bombing and wiring seem always to be on the programme now as we are going into the brick-fields where this is very necessary.

22 March 1916

I am on a court marshal, of which **Major Ffoulkes** of the Royal Scots is President, at the D.L.I. HQ. This is the first I have attended as a member and it naturally seems a little strange. Had tea with **Walmington** of the Durhams.

Y Company have been bathing at **Calonne.**

23 March 1916

After an hour's bombing and wiring, **Cohen** and I take the company past **Les Lauriers**, into the **Forêt de Nieppe.** It is a beautiful typically French wood with long straight 'rides'. Wood anemones and oxslips carpet the ground.* We pass near a shooting range labelled **Champ de Tir** and I go forward to see whether there is any chance of our running into a few stray bullets. It would be awfully infradig to be accidentally wounded.

In the afternoon throw my first bomb. Great and much bobbing of heads.

24 March, 1916

Major Hall, Company Commanders, Fricker and **Hardaker, Marshall** and myself are waiting at **Merville Station** for the motor bus to take us to the line, not the trenches which we were to have gone into but some near **Armentières**. The bus not being at the appointed place at 8.15, we sit in state in an estaminet drinking café in blessed ignorance of the fact that one is not allowed in at that hour.

10.15 no bus is here. We ring up Brigade who tell us that it will be here shortly and we must wait. Snow is falling and **Mason** is rather troublesome with his snowballs.

11.30 Notice comes that the bus cannot arrive so after our glorious wait we tramp home feeling disgusted with the world in general. We have to go at the same time tomorrow.

---

* He evidently knew the distinction between primroses *Primula vulgaris*, cowlips *P. veris* and the much less common oxlip *P. elatior*.

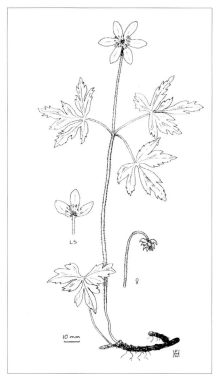
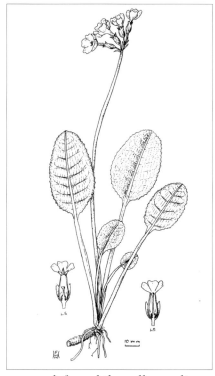

The white wood anemone Anemone nemorosa *left, and the yellow oxlip* Primula elatior *carpeted the ground of the Forêt de Dieppe.*

25 March 1916

Here we are again and the bus (these were London buses commandeered for British Expeditionary Force), has actually arrived to time. The regimental billeting officers also come with us as far as **Estaires**.

Bac St Maur later. We descend and walk to Brigade Headquarters and from there we are escorted down to the trenches, to be shown around by the 2nd Lincolns (Line Battalion). The Sniping Officer commands a company and the Intelligence Officer commands transport, the Bombing Officer also commands a company so we specialists generally escort ourselves round, questioning the men.

26 March 1916

We nearly always move on a Sunday. It must be our lucky day. Arrive at **Neuf-Berquin** disgusted we have only marched about two and a half miles and are billeting here for the night. It is a miserable little country village with its houses all on the main street. Billets are scarce and we have a rottenly draughty room.

Cohen and I are sleeping in one bed in a wee room in which there is hardly room to put our things.

The seconds in command of companies and the various specialists are to go and billet near the trenches. At 4.30pm I go with **Marshall** and the snipers.

I have just had tea. The snipers and **Marshall** have had orders from **Major Hall** to go straight on tonight. I am going to see the C.O. as I have had no intimation about going. I am vastly annoyed that I haven't been warned. 15 minutes later. The CO says I may go on in my own time in the morning. Cheers, this gives me a decent time in bed.

27 March 1916

I am delighted that I didn't go up yesterday as I am off on the blanket wagon to **Bac St Maur** thus saving me a trek of seven miles. It is gloriously hot and I arrive at the head of the Communication Trench in preparation. I meet Lincoln's C.O. halfway down through the trench and he says he will go through the Log Book with me.

Introduce myself to Y Company Headquarters, later will have a good lunch. Just now three whizz bangs have been unpleasantly near the dugout and we have retired into the fire trench, awaiting further developments. It is now deemed safe to return and finish our repast.

The Battalion arriving now (8.15pm) and I meet my Platoon at the entrance to **Dee Post** in which it is to be stationed for the next four days. All in, safe and sound, no casualties and duties told off. I return to rest in my little sleeping dugout. I have arranged to share the bed with **Cohen** who is now taking the watch. The Bed, so called, is merely two pieces of lath with rabbit wire stretched across but it is exceedingly comfortable.

28 March 1916

I have just awakened and find it is a 'stand to.' Why didn't **Cohen** waken me before? The bounder has been sleeping in the mess dugout on a chair. I feel awfully selfish having taken the bed all night, I must rig up another tomorrow or today if possible.

We make another bed and cover it with sandbags. Sandbags – wonderful things – we use them for everything i.e. for building breastworks and revetting, bedclothes, ration bags, post bags, covering for steel helmets and periscopes and all my clothes and kit are wrapped in them before being placed on my valise, in order to facilitate packing.

I have an interesting day with the snipers. 9.20 I have just come in from examining our wire and ditch and taken **Parker** and **Sergeant Burley.** In climbing over the parapet on my return, I catch the fleshy part of my leg above the knee on a bayonet but fortunately it is not deep. It is a wonder that we have not been fired on as the machine gunners, not knowing that we were out, were ready to let loose a few rounds on our shadowy forms. Someone has been careless in not informing them of the exit of a patrol. Not that our loss would have made much difference but it would be distinctly uncomfortable for us.

29 March 1916

8.30am. The enemy have just sent over some rifle grenades, I hate the things. We are busy retaliating. I bet the old Hun is chuckling up his sleeve as all ours are falling short and ten out of the fifteen are duds. Bless the munitioneers or perhaps it may be the damp ground.

30 March 1916

I have just spotted a large party of Germans through the telescope and have got the guns onto them. They have dispersed.

A beastly trench mortar fiend has turned up this afternoon and insists on pooping off a number of rounds, 60 pounders from two different places. I know what this means, he poops off, walks away and leaves the infantry to get the retaliation. Strafe trench [obscure] 2.30pm. The sixty pounders have just been fired. I knew we should have retaliation and the Hun is sending them over near **Bell's** dugout. Poor old **Bell** is in a fearful stew and 'nae wonder ah aye.'

31 March 1916

Very quiet day. We are being relieved today. I am going through the Log Book with the C.O.

8.30 we are relieved and making our way to the reserve billets.

1 April 1916

I have made an excellent [April] fool of **Huffam** and no one has made a fool of me.

Crawford is a capital Mess President and we are comfortably ensconced in a large empty farm, and **Rose** has lent us his gramophone.

Colbeck's billet has just been shelled and I am going to find out if possible the calibre and range.

Later. I have just sent a list to Division HQ.

2 April 1916

We are attending a service in a tent behind an old barn. We can't all get in but have to stand round and try to listen.

What a lovely afternoon! The sun is baking hot and **Cohen** and I are lounging around on an old hay rick eating toffee (a present from home) and watching aeroplanes. Everything is very quiet, perhaps that is because it is Sunday.

I am detailed to take my platoon on an R.E. fatigue tonight; **Redman** is also taking his.

12 midnight. I have just arrived from my working party. The men have been digging places for dugout frames and also carrying stuff across the open space between the support and firing lines. It was rather ticklish work and several times the Boche opened rapid fire at our front line, those bullets which missed the front parapet came very near to us and we had on several occasions to lie down. No one was hurt.

3 April 1916

I am ordered to proceed to **Sailly** billeting. My sergeants (I always take an N.C.O. from each company) are waiting at the cross-roads.

Arrangements are altered, I am to take the Adjutant's horse and draw money at the Field Cashier's Office at **Sailly.**

12.15. I am back with the money but learn that I am to go to **Estaires** for further orders re billeting. **Cross** wants his horse and I must perforce take **Huffam's** Jim. He provides me with two bits of excitement. He slings round on the pavé between an omnibus and hospital car going in opposite direction. There is much diverting of wheels, nearly a collision, sparks from the pavé and unprintable from the two drivers and myself.

A mule team takes fright over a canal draw-bridge and I am nearly three-quarters of the way over and can't get past. I have either to go back at ten miles per hour or swim in the canal.

It is quite all right. We have got out of it without a scratch but I can't quite make out how. I find that the billets are at **Nerf-Berquin,** beastly hole. I manage to get the billets fixed up somehow and arrive back in the dark at 8.30. I hear that I am to fix up for a quarter-master's store which I was told to leave out yesterday so I am to go again at six in the morning.

4 April 1916

The Battalion is coming along and I have just managed to get everything ready in time. It is quite a relief to find no one is cursing you, as the Billeting Officer usually gets it in the neck. He is not as a rule allowed enough time. The men are settling down and seem quite satisfied.

5 April 1916

The men are getting ready for an inspection tomorrow. **Cohen** and I take the opportunity of going to **La Gorgue** for a bath. These baths are occupied but we find some good Divisional baths in **Estaires.** The officers' compartments are big vats (cement) in a factory duly screened off. Very much refreshed. Tea at café.

6 April 1916

I hate inspection, always did and always shall. Everybody has turned out spick and span and I think **General Penny** is highly pleased with us.

We are moving again tomorrow but only to **Estaires**. Another brigade wants our billets.

At tea-time **Colonel Wear** calls to see me. Had a good chat about Headingley.

7 April 1916

Busy issuing cigarettes to my platoon. Mother has sent me a whole bundle and the men are very grateful. There is nothing in the British soldier's life better than Wild Woodbine. I can't say, though, that they particularly appeal to me.

8pm I have just come out of the Hippodrome at **Estaires.**

The Battalion moved here this afternoon at 2.30 and so everyone except **Huffam** has been to the pictures so does seem funny and it feels almost as if we were at Tidworth [military town in Wiltshire] again. Many people gave turns, notably **Jackson** who ventriloquised and **Percival** and **Shield** who gave a sparring exhibition. It certainly livens things up a bit.

8 April 1916

After rifle inspection **Cohen** and I go a short march whilst **Westcott** bombs.

The afternoon is taken up by a reconnaissance of the **Sailly** road in which I am assisted by **Marshall** and a few scouts. It is a long walk.

On the way back we call at some officers' tea-rooms and find them excellent; dainty sweets and chocolate liqueurs – we shall certainly go there again.

Norman Wootton has invited me to his mess but I am afraid it is too late to go.

9 April 1916

We have just had a bust up with **Huffam,** who paraded the company too early and consequently we were late. However, we have all been to a barn to church and have only just managed to squash the battalion in. The Padre gave us a few comic turns such as slipping off his tub etc.

This afternoon we have visited the tea-room again and this evening

Norman [Wootton] and **Cross** are here at a little dinner party.

10 April 1916
Just off for a march. It is a glorious morning and the hedges and blossom are full out. Really France looks quite pretty today.

Pay this afternoon and I learn that I am to go down to the trenches tomorrow to meet the people who are now in and get full particulars for when we go in on Wednesday.

11 April 1916
It seems very early. We are parading in the main street **Estaires** at 8am. We have met our guides at **Laventie** in a street wrecked and shattered out of recognition.

Cohen is in his dugout taking over from the 14th Gloucesters. **Capt. Williams** is a charming man who welcomes us and makes us extremely comfortable.

Taking over is not really a pleasant proceeding. Everyone looks upon it as a fearful bore and strange people come into your dugout and steal[?] your last meal which you were saving, as the mess has been packed up and already sent away.

I believe I have mentioned before that it always snows or rains when we take over. It is doing so now, raining hard.

12 April 1916
The usual routine of observation. A number of Germans were seen in the brick salient and I had quite an interesting ten minutes watching them.

13 April 1916
Much the same as yesterday. So far we have had only about two killed by snipers. In W Company hostile snipers are extremely active sniping many periscopes but further up the line they are indifferent shots.

14 April 1916
I have been up to Headquarters to try and fix up an O.P. but it won't do. Find that a number of people who are taking over from us are coming down and I shall have to take the sniping officer round with me.

3.0 still waiting. We shall give it up shortly. Make acquaintance of our new M.O. **Capt. Wilson**.

15 April 1916
We are relieved by the 10th South Wales Borderers of the Welsh Division.

Message has arrived down that I am to escort the two Brigadiers round. I march in front showing the chief points, aided by a No. 14 periscope (which appreciably magnified the front line). Half way down the line I provide a comedy turn by slipping off the duckboard into a drain. Dashed rotten, one feels an awful fool doing these things in front of a Brigadier.

10 o'clock pm. We are just passing through **Laventie** having been relieved. What a place! The main street is desolation, the moon shining through the skeleton of the church tower, the rows of houses with no roofs or merely charred rafters, the Convent mere outer walls all tended to give the place the weirdest and most creepy aspect. One could almost imagine ghosts.

16 April 1916

We are up betimes, 6 o'clock and find the men fast asleep, poor beggars, they are awfully tired and so are we all. We march at intervals of two minutes to **Croix Barbée**. I have to find garrisons for three posts and so take them off. There are no guides. The posts are easily found but the occupants evaded our notice until fairly late. The day passed on and we are still more tired.

17 April 1916

Our abode is a ruined house which has been a large farm, the men are billeted in one part and the officers in another. A socially disposed shell has deemed it good to call upon the occupants at one time or another and has entered the front door, leaving its card and my chambre couché in the form of charred and plasterless walls. There are no doors to the rooms. It is quite probable that these have found their way to the trenches as the village is unoccupied by civilians. The doorways and part of the walls are covered with sack cloth. The only furniture is a rough trestle table and two forms. I luckily have a bed. The draughts are some of the best to be found in France and are of several qualities, strong, fresh and mild. We rarely run short of them, in fact our fire burns away too quickly in the grate.

I have definitely taken the sniper area over today from **Marshall.** The C.O. has been lecturing us.

18 April 1916

Busy indenting for clothing etc for the snipers.

19 April 1916

Practically no parades today. Had a delightful bath at **Croix Barbée**. Just fancy bathing under shell fire.

20 April 1916

We parade at 7.30am and take orders from **Heaton** of the Durhams. The day is fairly quiet. At night we fix up loopholes etc. The snipers generally go in during the morning of relief so that other posts can be taken over during daylight and any special places of interest pointed out to them.

21 April 1916

Good Friday. Wet and horrible.

22 April 1916

Still wet and horrible; only a few grenades over. Our men bag two Germans. The C.O. seems fairly pleased with our work.

23 April 1916

Easter Sunday, and a beautiful day, too beautiful to be fighting. Just behind us are the remains of the once pretty village of **Neuve Chapelle**. The church is defunct, the houses around mere heaps of brick and yet above all as in innumerable cases stands the crucifix, unhurt.

24 April 1916

Am again handing over to **Heaton.**

Later. Have been out nearly a whole day, and have just had a delightful bath. I expected every minute a crump would land on the bath house and crump permitting I would have to run out 'with nothing on.' How awfully infradig.

25 April 1916

I am in No.2 Headquarters Mess now and **Harris** gives me notice as he wishes to remain with C Company amongst his friends.

There is quite a good garden to this billet and we spend our time reading amongst the flowers. No.2 Mess is composed of **Eric Fricker**, OC Lewis Groups; **DeWitt**, OC Bombers and myself.

26 April 1916

Cohen comes in to dinner at night. **Cohen** and I take the others on at cards and we win.

27 April, 1916

Am detailed to make a reconnaissance this morning and take **Fricker** with me. During the afternoon a note comes from the Adjutant that the Brigade Major is very pleased with my sketch and report and wants me to do another. I carry on straight away. One report deals with sirens and the second with emergency roads.

I dine with Y Company. An artillery strafe is supposed to come off tonight but nothing has happened so far.

28 April 1916
We move to **Les Lobes**. I am relieved at 12 noon by snipers of the 17 Lancashire Fusiliers. Meet **Fricker** and **DeWitt** who have also been relieved. We march straight to **Les Lobes** and spend the afternoon in looking for a No.2 Mess. We find it at about 6pm.

I hear that poor old **Cohen** is wounded. I wonder if it is a blighty. He was wounded just outside our old billet at **Croix Barbée.**

29 April 1916
During the afternoon **DeWitt** and myself venture on a motor wagon into **Béthune** bent on purchasing a gramophone. We have now obtained an excellent one and some records. We shall have <u>some</u> mess now. We ride part of the way back in a motor bus and later whilst we are walking the remainder of the way **DeWitt** sees **Gen. Penny** in his car and nearly drops the gramophone in his anxiety to salute.

30 April 1916
Of course as we knew, the mess is flooded with people listening to our new acquisition.

1 May 1916
Hoggett drills my men and I am content.

2 May 1916
We are writing out schemes for an attack on a farm. Much sweating of the brow. Great sketches.

3-4 May, 1916
We have a concentration march to **Calonne** and **Paradis.**

5 May 1916
I am detailed to fetch a draft from **Lestrem** and am off on my horse. Later. Am searching high and low for the new men but cannot find them anywhere. A Sherwood officer is also looking for his men. After much searching and riding and telegraphing from Division I find that the draft has arrived in billets by the light railway. It has been a waste of afternoon espe-

cially as the horse has been damned stupid and would shy at everything.

I find that I have had the Brigade Intelligence job offered to me but the Colonel would not let me go.

6 May 1916

Off early to the Line today, this time to **Richebourg Sector.** There is no proper dugout in the **Rue du Bois** which is a more unhealthy place than the front line so we go up and mess with Y Company.

7 to 9 May 1916

Much happens the same each day. Sniping continually. The Hun keeps down well here and one doesn't get much chance of a decent shot.

10 May 1916

I am relieved and march back to billets after having first escorted two Generals, two Brigade Majors, a Colonel and a string of others round the Lines; what a notable procession; why doesn't the Hun put a pip-squeak over?

I have to reconnoitre posts in the back areas so that we shall know where our alarm posts are.

11 May 1916

Luxury. I have a bath.

We look round **Richebourg** church from where **Winston Churchill** watched the battle of **Neuve Chapelle**. Only pillars and a few walls remain standing. The big bronze bells lie in a terrible mess up on the ground among broken rafters and near the tower door is a large unexploded Jack Johnson. In the churchyard itself are many shell holes, some appearing nearly large enough to bury the remains of the church itself in, and all over the graves have been torn asunder by force of the explosions and gaunt skeletons are visible, and a thigh bone here, and a finger there. If the inhabitants were to come back now they would indeed weep for the bodies of their dear ones strewn about.

I hear that poor old **Crawford** has been killed in Bute Post shortly after I had been speaking to him.

12 May onwards, 1916

A bus is picking up four snipers and myself and a few others from the Division to proceed on a sniping course at **Steenbecque,** near **Hazebrouck.**

I arrive at Corps Sniping School and we are living in a little farmhouse, a cosy little place with an oak ceiling and an open fireplace. A row of pewter plates and jugs adorn the mantelshelf and the room is just big enough for our mess. My bedchamber opens onto the mess – and I have real sheets and a beastly lace canopy, like that on a baby's cradle, above my head.

The Commandant (a 'Loot') says that he wants this to be more of a rest than anything, and when the work which isn't very strenuous is finished, one can go anywhere. I pay a visit to **Hazebrouck** one day.

The country is beautiful and we are nestled at the foot of a wood and at night the air is a perpetual hum of the croaking of bullfrogs. It is like half a dozen corncrakes in a singing competition.

19 May 1916

I return for duty and hear that **Mason** has been wounded. He was standing on the duckboard and bending over looking in a dugout doorway and a whizz bang caught him bending.

20 May 1916

Great excitement, the Huns have brought down one of our aeroplanes behind the front line and now our artillery are smashing it up.

21 May 1916

The Daylight Savings Bill came into force in England today. They will all be getting up an hour earlier.

22 May 1916

We march to **Croix Marmeuse** and are going to mess with Z Company. What a crowd in a mess. Our gramophone is in great demand.

We are being inspected by the **Archbishop of Canterbury** [the Archbishop of Canterbury in 1916 was **Randall Thomas Davidson**] who seems to be quite a nice old boy but we are rather annoyed at having to form up, just after a march and listen to speeches. However, he gives us England's blessing and thanks so we let him off lightly.

23 to 26 May 1916

A period of training in range firing at the **Nieppe Forest Range** and sand-bagging, lopping etc in the vicinity of our billets.

27 May 1916

I am suddenly rushed off to reconnoitre the route to **Festubert** as an attack is expected. Arrive back after cycling like blaizes at 2.30. I don't suppose we shall have to move, we often have these scares.

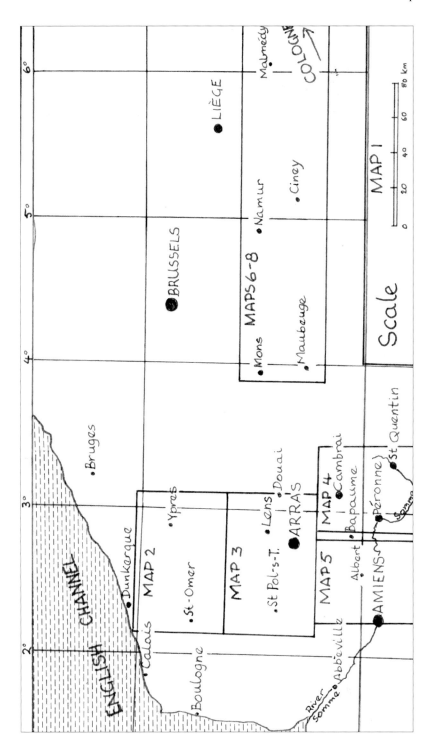

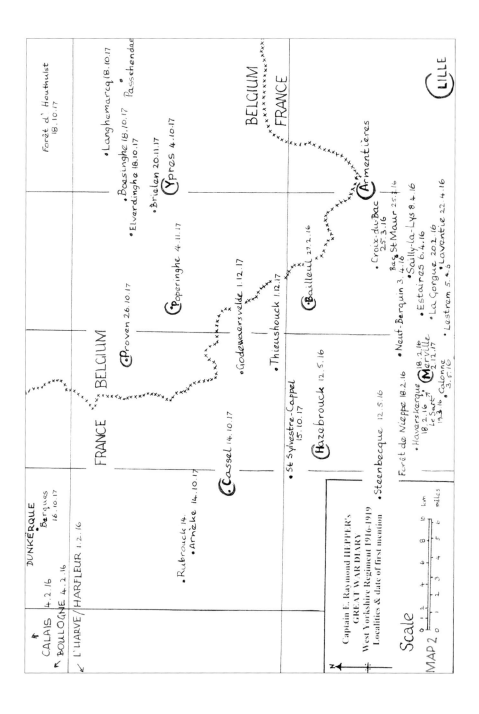

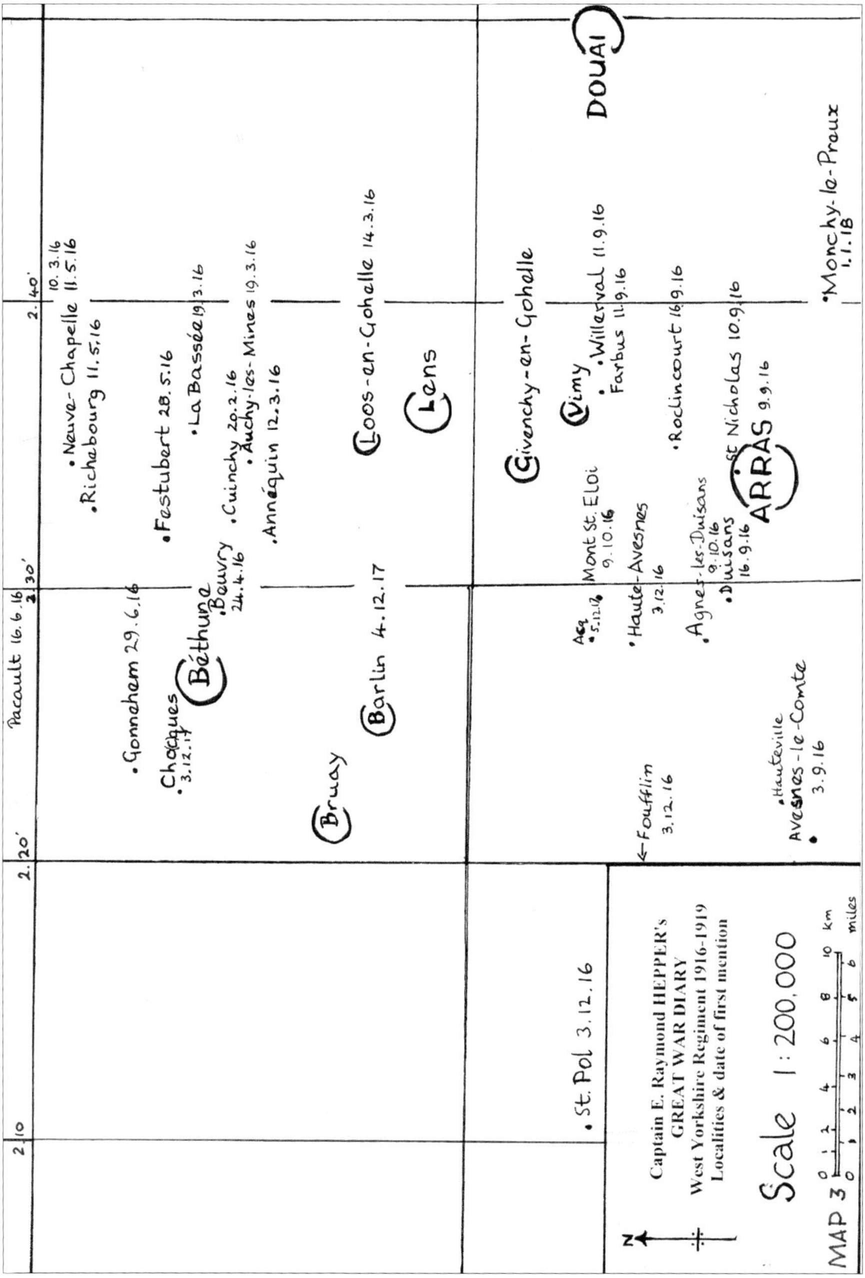

Paccault 16.6.16

10.3.16
• Neuve - Chapelle
• Richebourg 11.5.16 11.5.16

• Festubert 28.5.16
• La Bassée 19 3.16
• Gonnehem 29.6.16 • Cuinchy 20.2.16
Chocques • Auchy-les-Mines 19.3.16
3.12.17 Béthune
• Beuvry • Annéquin 12.3.16
24.4.16

Loos-en-Gohelle 14.3.16

(Bruay)
(Barlin 4.12.17) (Lens)

Givenchy-en-Gohelle

(Vimy) • Willerval 11.9.16
Acq Mont St. Eloi Farbus 11.9.16
• 5.12.16 9.10.16
• Haute-Avesnes • Roclincourt 16.9.16
3.12.16
Agnez-les-Duisans ST Nicholas 10.9.16
9.10.16 (ARRAS) 9.9.16
• Duisans
16.9.16

• Monchy-la-Preux
1.1.18

DOUAI

← Foufflin • St. Pol 3.12.16
3.12.16

• Hauteville
Avesnes-le-Comte
• 3.9.16

Captain E. Raymond HEPPER's
GREAT WAR DIARY
West Yorkshire Regiment 1916-1919
Localities & date of first mention

Scale 1: 200,000

0 1 2 3 4 5 6 7 8 9 10 km
0 1 2 3 4 5 6 miles

N →
MAP 3

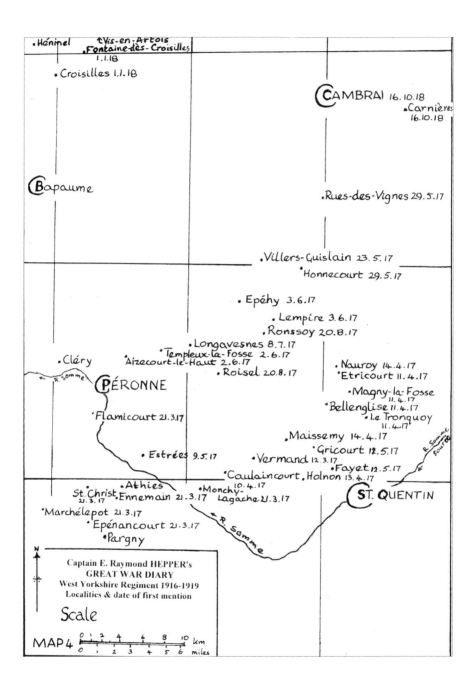

.Héninel   tVis-en-Artois
        .Fontaine-dès-Croisilles
              1.1.18

.Croisilles 1.1.18

CAMBRAI 16.10.18
                    .Carnières
                      16.10.18

Bapaume

.Rues-des-Vignes 29.5.17

.Villers-Guislain 23.5.17
        ˙Honnecourt 29.5.17

. Epéhy 3.6.17

        . Lempire 3.6.17
        .Ronssoy 20.8.17

        .Longavesnes 8.7.17
    ˙Templeux-la-Fosse 2.6.17
.Cléry   ˙Aizecourt-le-Haut 2.6.17
R.Somme   .Roisel 20.8.17

                    . Nauroy 14.4.17
                    ˙Etricourt 11.4.17

PÉRONNE

                    .Magny-la-Fosse
                          11.4.17
                    ˙Bellenglise 11.4.17
                        .Le Tronquoy
                            11.4.17

˙Flamicourt 21.3.17

                    .Maissemy 14.4.17
                    ˙Gricourt 12.5.17
    . Estrées 9.5.17   .Vermand 12.3.17
                        .Fayet 12.5.17
            ˙Caulaincourt .Holnon 13.4.17

        .Athies   .Monchy-
                      10.4.17
St.Christ.Ennemain 21.3.17 Lagache 21.3.17
    21.3.17
                                        ST. QUENTIN
˙Marchélepot 21.3.17
        . Epénancourt 21.3.17   R. Somme
            .Pargny

N

Captain E. Raymond HEPPER's
GREAT WAR DIARY
West Yorkshire Regiment 1916-1919
Localities & date of first mention

Scale

MAP 4   0 1 2 4   6   8   10 km
        0   1   2   3   4   5 6 miles

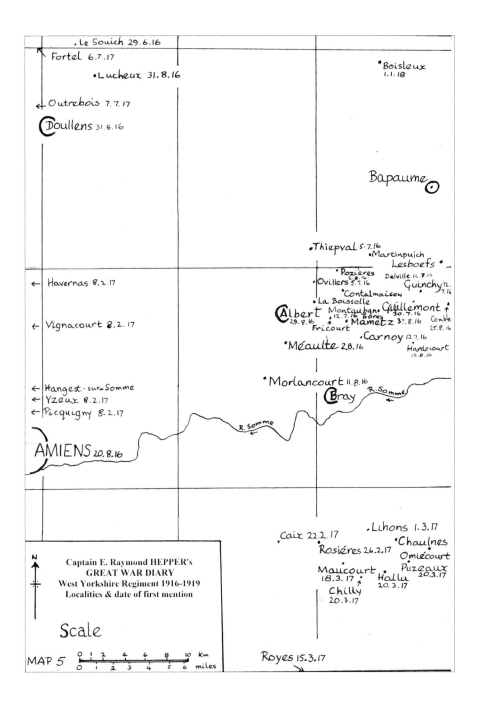

. Le Souich 29.6.16
Fortel 6.7.17
     • Lucheux 31.8.16
                               • Boisleux
                                 1.1.18
← Outrebois 7.7.17
Ⓓoullens 31.6.16

                       Bapaume ⊙

                •Thiepval 5.7.16
                       •Martinpuich
                            Lesboefs •
← Havernas 8.2.17   •Pozières Delville 12.7.16
                  •Ovillers 5.7.16   Guinchy 12.
                       •Contalmaison   7.16
                 • La Boisselle Guillemont
← Vignacourt 8.2.17   Ⓐlbert Montauban• 30.7.16
                      •12.7.16 Foney   Comble
               29.8.16   •Mametz 31.8.16 25.8.16
               Fricourt
                     •Carnoy 12.7.16
         •Méaulte 2.8.16   Hardecourt
                          12.8.16

         •Morlancourt 11.8.16
← Hangest-sur-Somme
← Yzeux 8.2.17   Ⓑray R.Somme
← Picquigny 8.2.17

                    R. Somme
ⒶMIENS 20.8.16

                       •Lihons 1.3.17
            •Caix 22.2.17   •Chaulnes
                Rosiéres 26.2.17 Omiécourt
N   Puzeaux
↑   Captain E. Raymond HEPPER's Maucourt •   20.3.17
✛   GREAT WAR DIARY   18.3.17 • Hallu
   West Yorkshire Regiment 1916-1919   20.3.17
    Localities & date of first mention   Chilly
                       20.3.17

Scale

MAP 5 0 1 2 4 6 8 10 Km
       0 1 2 3 4 5 6 miles   Royes 15.3.17

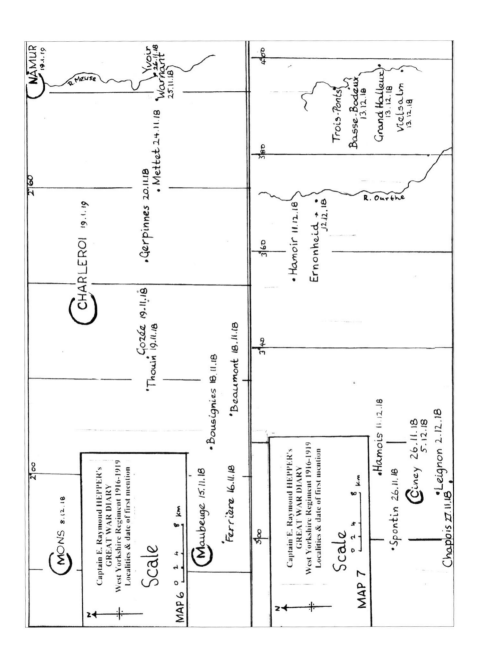

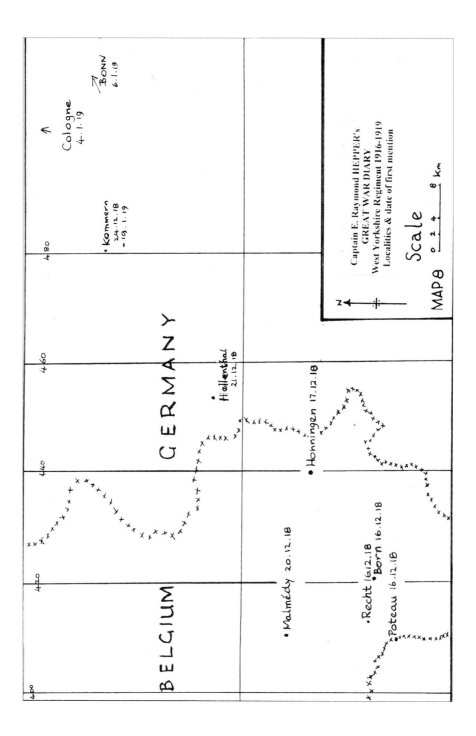

28 May 1916

By Jove, we have to move and we are parading at 5.30 to march to the trenches or islands at **Festubert** where we take over from the King's Royal Rifles.

29 May 1916

Finding my way round the sniping posts. We have a great many more to put in so I shall have plenty to do. It seems fairly quiet.

30 May 1916

6pm. A bombardment has started. Great Scott! I have never seen such a sight before. Heavens! shrapnel, and all kinds of weird shells. This lasts for about an hour. There is the rattle of machine guns and all quietens down.

We learn next day that the old Boche has been over and taken thirty Notts and Derby's prisoners and also two officers – glad it wasn't us.

All the specialists have a beastly time with trench mortars in the Com[munications] Trench. All the so-called trenches we have been into, with the exception of those we saw south of the canal, have been breast-worked and these breast-works at **Festubert** form a number of isolated islands which can only be reached during the day in a few instances by crawling on one's stomach, and so the garrison is isolated during the day.

31 May 1916

Great sport sniping from one of my posts. A German is trying to locate us and is using a dummy to attract our fire. We ignore this and finally hit the other sniper, whether I have merely wounded him or whether he is dead I do not know but both **Blower** who is observing it and I saw him fall. A few minutes afterwards our place is being heavily peppered. We clear out.

1 June 1916

We are relieved and march to **Le Touret.**

2 June 1916

A number of the Boys came in after dinner. We have a piano which is a great luxury in these parts even though it is out of tune. **Redman** and **Wilkinson** entertain, I recite but make an awful fool of myself, and others perform.

We have a few Gloucesters attached to us for instruction. They are good fellows.

2 and 4 June 1916

I am attached to a battery of field guns for two days and learn a few things.

6 June 1916

I return to the trenches. Poor old **Hitchen** has just been killed while going out on patrol. **Kavanagh** and one of the raiders also killed.

7 and 8 June 1916

The usual trench intelligence routine.

9 June 1916

I am sitting in **Rose's** dark dugout, after having had a visit to my posts, where somebody strange calls "How's Wood Lane" [Headingley, Leeds]. I find it is **B. Midgley** who has joined us for a few days on a Cook's Tour.

10 June 1916

I've got another Boche today.

11 June 1916

Relieved the 17th K.R.R. and met **Ewing** who was on a sniping course with me.

12 June 1916

March to **Croix Marmeuse,** arriving there about 3am.

13 to 15 June 1916

Training and resting.

16 June 1916

Singer, our new interpreter, and I are off on cycles to billet the battalion at **Hingette (Hinges?).** We have just finished and put everyone in splendidly when we find there is another move in the morning and we have to set off at once to re-billet in **Béthune.**

    Béthune billets successfully arranged and are instructed that we may stay the night and meet the battalion in the morning. **Hoggett** brings me a message from the C.O. stating that the battalion will not come tomorrow but the day after so **Singer** and I are to have a good day in **Béthune** on our own.

17 June 1916

Good, we have the whole day before us and so get up at eleven.

    Later. Have just seen **Hoggett** who informs us that the battalion is on its way, arrangements having been altered.

At 3pm. They arrive and there is some comic business with the Y Company whose billet has been taken by the Cheshires.

I spend from 3pm until 8.30 looking for officers' billets for **Huffam** & co. The men have now ample accommodation in the barracks.

18 June 1916
We walk round the town and examine the old buildings.

19 June 1916
After the parade we go down to the swimming baths and have a swim. A fair number of the other officers are there and we arrange to make it a daily exercise. We then partake of chocolates and sweets.

We realise what a wonderful billet we have; it is a fairly large house in **Rue d'Aire** [in **Béthune**] and it is the property of a French colonel who wishes British officers to receive the same treatment as if it had been himself. He has left us a French cook and a housemaid who prepare all meals for us in the approved French style. We have a large dining room, a music room with piano, and a beautiful bedroom which **DeWitt** has collared. I am sleeping in a house a little further up the road. I understand **DeWitt** is leaving shortly so I shall come in for his room.

20 to 22 June 1916
Parades, bathing and chocolates as arranged.

23 June 1916
The C.O. has been invited to dinner tonight. He arrives with the adjutant and we have a topping little dinner followed by music. He looks at me and politely asks why I haven't given him the best billet. I fortunately have been studying a reply for this natural question all the afternoon and when given rather clears the air.

I append the dinner menu on that memorable occasion:

> Potage aux Bethunois
> Soles aux gratin a la Lewis Gun (**Fricker** is our Lewis Gun Officer)
> Canetons roti aux pois Bautanes
> Asperges Walker; Sauce Blanche (**Walker** is a long thin officer)
> Fraise sniper aux victimes (which is my job and explains itself)
> Café et liqueur si martial
> Orchestra Krupp (heavy guns rolling in the distance)

We are all very excited and wonder what is going to happen as the Great Offensive starts today. We expect to move shortly.

26 June 1916

What a night. Everyone is in. **DeWitt** is going to **England** and bliss tomorrow. We have a roaring time and everyone makes speeches etc.

27 June 1916

106th Brigade Transport Show. The West Yorks take five 1sts out of 6. Well done **Hardaker.**

28 June 1916

During the last few days we have been in Corps and G.H.Q. Reserve but we believe we are now going into the Line somewhere in the vicinity of **Arras**.

TO THE SOMME BATTLEFIELD, June 1916

29 June 1916

I am detailed to parade a Brigade Headquarters at **Gonnehem** immediately, with my billeting sergeants. The Battalion is moving at a moment's notice. People are flying round, gramophone being packed up.

Sergeant Lyne late, much fluent English. We finally arrive at Brigade having jumped on a motor wagon and report to new Brigade Major. We are to wait for a lorry. One hour later – here it is and we pack in, we shall have to buck up as the battalion will be leaving by train in two hours.

1pm. We arrive at our destination which we presume is just behind the line. It seems very quiet tonight.

Old **Sutherland** is here and we ask where are we. It appears we are about 25 miles from the line and are to billet at a little place called **Le Souich** near **Doullens**.

1 to 4 July 1916

In this pretty village of **Le Souich** we billet in the dark after having turned out the Maire to show us round and wake up the inhabitants. The Battalion arrives at 10am. Everyone seems pretty satisfied. The great offensive started on July 1st.

5 July 1916

We leave **Le Souich,** in a motor lorry and reach a camp in the **Bois de Warremont** west of **Thiepval** and **Ovillers**, and see the remains of the

Leeds Pals (15 West Yorks) who are just passing through. We understand that they went too far in their attack on July 1st, and the Boche came up behind them. Whatever the story is, they were very badly hit in the taking of **Serre.**

7 July 1916
Several of us have just been into **Anthee,** a village about two miles away to buy strawberries. We were told after searching high and low that the only place to get them would be at the chateau now used as a hospital. We troop up. An old housekeeper opens the door and we find that this part of the house is not a hospital but is occupied by the French owner. We were ushered into a room and presently a charming girl tells us that the housekeeper is getting our strawberries.

I converse in French! with the girl, **Best** chipping in occasionally in English which to our amazement we find she knows to a certain extent. I hope we haven't said anything we ought not to have said. The strawberries having arrived, we regretfully take our leave. We are begged to accept the strawberries as a gift and so we say farewell to our Young French Lady of the Chateau.

8 July 1916
Major Gill and a few others saw **Col. Moore**, one of our old C.Os. He calls this afternoon to see the old battalion again.

9 July 1916
On the trek. We pass **Bresle** and cross the **River Somme**.

10 July 1916
Arrive at **Bois Celestines** where we are in huts in the wood. The French have a number of camps in the adjoining woods, down in the valley, for we are now fairly high above the winding **River Somme** and we are in the back areas of the **Somme Battlefields.**

11 July 1916
We march from **Bois Celestines** to **Billone Wood** and bivouac in a field behind some 12 inch howitzers. We are under the impression that we are very much nearer the Boche than we actually are.

12 July 1916
We enter **Carnoy valley** and bivouac in the **Talus Boise** a long strip of wood running up the valley towards **Montauban**. We meet **Colonel Moore**

who is in charge of a new normal gauge railway line in the course of construction.

How strange everything appears. This is our first experience of any offensive. We find that we are camped just in front of a battery of sixty pounder guns and a row of 9.2cm French trench mortars. These are after the type of the old Crimean Naval Guns and are mounted on wooden carriages and adapted with breach loaders. They are set by tapping the carriage into the required position. A string is pulled and the field gun blowing out our candles[?] and at the same time rolling over. Much amusement is caused by the heaving and crow-barring required to replace them in position for firing anew. **Guillemont** was their objective 7,700 yards away. On the other side of the valley are one or two squadrons of Indian Cavalry awaiting their turn. Much excitement prevails and we conclude that we are going to win the war.

The next day or two are spent in working parties re **Welches** and **Colbeck** being wounded in **Montauban** and **Trônes Wood** respectively. The remaining officers repair daily to hear orders being made and cancelled at the brigade – 'We are to attack **Guinchy** this way' and then 'that way' several times a day.

The Indian Cavalry. Traditional cavalry with lances was very vulnerable to machine guns and modern artillery. Hundreds of thousands of war horses were still required for other duties on the battlefield. By permission of the Imperial War Museum (neg. no. Q824). See 13-14.5.17.

Finally we receive definite orders and I am to proceed at 3.30pm to **Delville Wood** to tape out the starting points for the great attack on **Guinchy**. An order has just come through cancelling this tape laying, much to my joy, but why cancel when everything seems plane [i.e. plain] sailing at last? Why? – because the Boche has retaken the greater part of **Delville Wood** in which we were to form up.

This map is deceptive in as much as all the villages appear to be flourishing [map not clear enough to reproduce].

East of **Albert:**

Every village is a heap of ruins and every wood has the appearance of a mass of broken telegraph poles.

'The blue' line gives the approximate British and French line on this date.

British north of **Hardecourt.**

French south of **Hardecourt.**

Brown = high ground

The following days are spent chiefly in the vicinity of **South Montauban Trench** on the outskirts of the village of that name. This trench is taped down by 5.9s and the C.O. and I have only escaped from two five yards away by throwing ourselves flat upon the ground.

Upon the next page [photograph not reproduceable] is the sunken road across which the trench passes; I have a little shelter in the road just above the white rail on the right side. Last night I was very tired and was in a heavy sleep when a shell burst in the road four yards away, wounding a passing man badly in the leg, a piece of shell at the same time cutting through sandbags of the shelter and passing about two inches from my body. I did not wake until I heard the shrieks of the wounded man whilst his wounds were being dressed.

I am sent up into **Montauban** village to liaise with the 9th Brigade. My Battalion is attached to that Brigade as an attack is to be made in **Delville Wood**.

The attack is unsuccessful, and our Battalion is not called upon.

Another brigade is relieving and I am still in liaison, ready to charge off to my Battalion with the order 'reinforce' and the plan for so-doing.

I am ensconced in a roomy German dugout with **Corporal Blower** and **Hunter** my servant. I understand this place was a German artillery head-quarters and it consists of several apartments. The walls are lined with field grey cloth with strips of panelling. Cupboards are inserted at convenient places and a quaint three-cornered bench fits the wall. There is a plentiful supply of purloined chairs and lounge seats. The gentle Hun at any rate knows how to make himself comfortable with other peoples' goods.

I have lost all count of dates as so many events are crowded into each day that it is difficult to tell where one ends and another begins. I had another escape yesterday. **Blower** suggested I might be more comfortable in a dugout a little higher up the road. I noticed a small crack in the roof and climbed up on top to see why and found that at some time a 5.9 had landed on top, scattering the covering earth so that should another happen along there would not be much protection. I decided to remain in my own place. A few hours later a shell landed in the doorway of that dugout completely demolishing it. I bless my powers of observation for spotting that wee crack in the roof.

22? July 1916

It is about 11.30pm and the Colonel and I go forward with the Battalion to **Bernafay Trench** running through the valley from **Bernafay Wood** to **Waterlot Farm**. The Battalion is stowed away in this trench which is really a communication trench, with crumps and other unpleasant things falling around. All the shell-holes appear to have a number of dead in them, mostly killed Scotchmen. A gigantic Scotchman and a German are locked together in a deadly embrace.

I am instructed to report to our own Brigade Headquarters a little further down **Caterpillar Valley** in a quarry.

12 mid-night. I arrive there and find the whole of brigade headquarters piled up in a little gallery in the quarry. The Assistant Staff Captain, the Brigade Major, the Acting Intelligence Officer, the Bombing Officer and last but not least the Brigadier piled practically on top of one another, surrounded by signallers and runners. All are trying to catch a short sleep before morning which would bring Heaven knows what. I manage to squeeze my slim? figure into the doorway and await events.

The whole Brigade is digging itself in **Caterpillar Valley.**

During the morning a tremendous barrage put down by the enemy is causing a number of casualties. Of course, the Boche knows all about the quarry and lands his 4.2s, 5.9s, 8 inch and other cheerful variety of shells into this place, 'mightily putting the wind up us.'

Just a word on cooks here. Is the mess cook a naturally brave man by nature of his job? In the heaviest bombardment you will find the cook slowly stirring his soup or frizzling bacon oblivious of the fact that shells are flying about. He is always the man who lights a smoky fire to draw the attention of the enemy. If there is a piece of tin or even a sandbag, he believes that he is perfectly [safe] though there is no protection whatever. I remember in one case in a bombardment, three men took shelter in a latrine with a corrugated iron roof, two got in comfortably and the third could only get his head in, all the rest was sticking out ostrich fashion and yet they all thought they were safe; the beauty of it was that a good cubby hole was situated in a bank not five yards away. This, however, is beside the point.

A number of men are killed or wounded and **Hamilton** and one or two other officers go off to the dressing station.

We are relieved in the evening and return to bivouacs in **Caftet Wood** where I join a tent with **Padre Bell.**

29 July 1916

After a short rest at **Caftet**, I am on my way to tape out a road from **Briguetesil-Maricourt** road to **South Bernafay Trench** which our battalion is to file into, to support the 30th Division. **Corporal Blower** and two other men are with me. Having done this, that is to place a tape from the artillery track to the trench so that it will be seen at night, we return to **Caftet Wood** and find the battalion ready to march up into the **Dublin Trench.**

Later. We are settled in the **Dublin Trench** and the trench just behind called **Casement**. I am in a little cubby hole with **Fricker.** We have orders to move up into **Bernafay Trench** to support the 30th Division in their attack from **Maltzhorn Ridge** in the morning. The enemy is putting a number of gas shells over and round the trench and many have gone down gassed. **Fricker** being a Lewis Gunner has been supplied with one of the new box respirators. I have my old P.H. Helmet.

Poor **Dykes**, brother of the man in Helmsley's shop, Headingley, has his head blown off.

We move. The Colonel, **Cross, Fricker** and myself followed by a few of Headquarters and the runners are going up into the front line preparatory to the attack.

30 July 1916

'Goodbye boys. A wee tot more of rum. Cheerioh' and over the top the 12th Battalion of the King's Liverpool Regiment go. All men smoking cigarettes and one can hardly realise that a proper attack is in progress.

What a day! Enfiladed heavily, we are waiting for the moment to support. I am sent by **Capt Rose** to bring the Battalion into the front line or what was the front line a short while ago. I take **Blower** with me with the instruction that if either of us is knocked out the message is to go straight on. There is a frightful smoke in the valley and shells are bursting round. We both know the place we are to go to and in our hurry forget the barrage and the smoke which nearly makes us lose our way. We arrive at **Bernafay**

Trench – what a sight, the sunken road near the trench is strewn with dead men and equipment. Horror and horror. The barrage has been put down along the road. I deliver my message and find **Fricker** arriving on the scene.

One of us has to carry the message back to the Colonel while the other brings up the Battalion. This falls to my lot. The remainder of the day is spent in a little shaft in which four of us are sitting on the steps. Pigeon baskets and other apparatus fills this up as well – and the barrage continues to fall all along the trench. God – this is awful. Shall we ever get out alive?

I believe I wrote a short note home a few minutes ago on a scrap of paper to relieve my feelings but whether I shall post it remains to be seen.

This afternoon **Fricker** has been brought down wounded, on a stretcher, he was guiding the battalion when he was hit in the hip and badly wounded. Thanks to **Best**, I do not think he will lose his leg. (For this good work **Fricker** gains the MC. I am also recommended but unfortunately don't get it.)

We do not support as we have not been called upon, but are holding the starting point in case old Boche counter attacks. News is slowly filtering back – an officer of the Liverpools – then a runner and so on. No one is in front of us except a small post. The attack has failed and only a few of those who left this trench this morning have got back. Only about forty. Poor brave Lads, Liverpool Pals Battalion.

We are warned that the Boche are preparing a large counter attack and massing troops in the neighbourhood of **G(u)illemont.** No attack has at present developed.

It is useless putting into writing the sights I have seen today for they will ever be in my mind as a momento of July 30.

Lieut. Keeton carried a note from Brigade Headquarters and after delivering the note through a heavy barrage he is injured by a shell. He obtains the MC.

31 July 1916
We have been relieved but I am too dazed to remember how. We have taken up our abode in **Caftet Wood** again.

1 August, 1916
The Battalion masses to move off to **Sandpit Valley**. A German aeroplane is high above us; in about two minutes the German artillery put over a number of 5.9s. The first one is unpleasantly near. I throw myself down behind a barrel, as if that was any use, and when I get up the barrel is filled to the brim with earth from the gaping shell hole next to it. Several times lately I

have proved that it is safer to be five or six yards from a shell than fifteen as the bursting power of the H.E. is upwards at first. One has unfortunately to contend with concussion.

Another is a blind i.e. one that does not explode, and if it had burst it would have killed or wounded the majority of the company; it came down directly on to one of the men cutting him completely in half. Never, I believe, has a battalion moved off so quickly. Everyone, I know, wanted to bolt and it was only strict discipline that kept the battalion in hand. I am sure I wanted to bolt more than anyone.

2 onwards, August 1916
Sandpit Valley. We have been here for several days in tents and in the distance can see the German shells bursting in **Pozières.** I believe we took this the other day.

The time is chiefly taken up in marching the men to bathe at **Méaulte.**

The Prince of Wales has just been into the camp. **Huffam** has been presented to him in the D.L.I. camp. **Huffam,** by the way, is temporarily commanding the D.L.I.

3? August 1916
We are now at **Morlancourt** a few miles further back and rumour has it that we are to go back for a long rest as we have been in the battle area for three weeks and lost nearly half our men.

6 August, 1916
At last we are here. This is the prettiest little place we have been to, as yet, and I know that we are going to have a good time. The Maire's son speaks a little English and thinks very highly of the British troops.

11 August 1916
Our stay here has not been very long and we are marching off again to the **Somme Battle Area.** This is a little disappointing but c'est la guerre.

Note: I am now Sniping, Intelligence, Lewis Gun, Signalling and Battalion officer and in charge of Headquarters Company.

We entrain at **Hang(u)est**, near **Picguiny** and arrive at **Morlancourt** during the night.

For a month I have not been billeting. I think this is the first time I have not been.

The flies are legion this year and the tables in the cottages are black with them. One cannot sleep at night for the swarms around ones head.

16 August 1916

We move to **Sandpit Valley**.

18 August 1916

We bivouac in **Contour Wood**, a little copse on the hill above **Caftet Wood** and not far from **Billone Wood** our first halting place on the **Somme**.

I am ordered to reconnoitre the trenches in the vicinity of **Arrowhead Copse**, beyond the **Maltzhorn Trench**, which is at present being held by the 105 Brigade. We shall presently take these trenches over. The day has been glorious and the Boche has not shelled much. We do not dawdle, however.

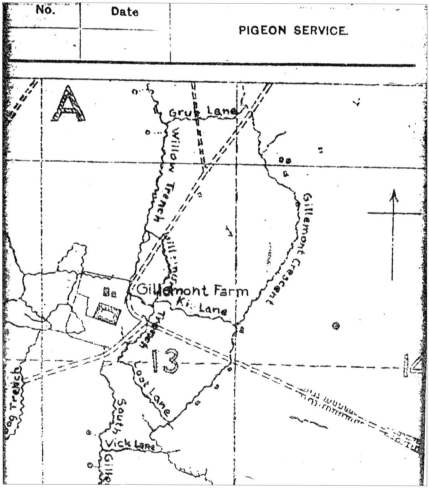

This map drawn by Raymond Hepper from an aerial photograph, was sent to the general by pigeon post - pigeon baskets cluttered the trenches, according to the diary entry of 30 July 1916.

22 August 1916
General Pinney has been over today and the jist of his speech was that we were 'lucky fellows' as we have to attack in a day or so.

23 August 1916
I mark out Company Areas in **Silesia Trench** and guide the Battalion there at night. Everything satisfactory.

24 August 1916
We are 'taking over' tonight, the Headquarters go up **Champagne Trench**, in the **Maltzhorn valley**, to confer with the Brigade which is established in its advanced Headquarters here. Boche is not very active in the valley but is shelling a battery in the wood in the French line. It is rather interesting watching the French gunners firing their shot and then running for cover from the return shell which is sure to come.

A French aeroplane has just crashed, a wing shot off, and the man has fallen out in mid air. This is the first time I have seen an aeroplane 'arched with success' with the exception of one brought down in flames over **Mametz.**

A battery of 75s is about twenty yards away from us drum firing and the noise is appalling. **Andy the cook** prepares us some tea and bread. We find ourselves taking over not the sector we had to reconnoitre but the trench further south called **Lonely Trench**. We are relieving the D.L.I. and during the relief I have one of the most unpleasant experiences I have yet had. By some mismanagement, or perhaps there is no other trench, both relief and relieving use the same communication trench and a jam is caused at a trench junction. Neither party can move either way and if the Hun had only the sense to put a few shells over he could scupper the lot of us. However, after a good deal of wriggling, during which **Captain Bell** who is extraordinarily fat, tries to get down a cable trench fifteen inches wide, and swearing [at] the seething mob with the aid of the sound of whistling shells overhead and the thought of what would happen if one fell short, manage to extricate ourselves and we arrive at our Battalion HQ dugout none the worse though a little tired.

25 August 1916
The enemy cannot be seen as his trenches lie in the hollow. In the distance at the other side of the valley **Leuze Wood** and **Le Forest** can be seen and above that ridge is the top of the spire of **Combles** Church.

I make several trips with **Blower** to the front line and this is by no means pleasant. The ground around is littered with dead and the flies are atrocious.

My battalion buries them at nightfall.

During the evening the enemy violently bombards us both in the front line and in the assembly trench. I get vastly excited and we all think old Boche is coming over; though I cannot say why, we all fervently wish he would. We see the SOS put up from the front line and we are all prepared for him. **Bell** has instructions to counterattack on the front line if the Hun attacks it and this he quickly does though he mistakes our support line for the front line and I very nearly shoot him as we are expecting Germans and not British. After the bombardment, when things quieten down, I go with **Blower** to the front line to ascertain what has happened. This little trip is very exciting as we are not quite sure who we may find in the line, and the bombardment has so demolished what bit of communication trench there was, that in the blackness of the night we are not sure whether we shall walk into the German line or not. The first person we run into is very surprised to see my revolver in his ribs and bursts out an unmistakable English oath, so we find that we have not strayed.

26 August 1916

We are still in the bally old trench though things have considerably quietened down. We heard that poor old **Stead** has been killed during the bombardment yesterday. He was a great favourite. **Forshaw** has also gone down with shell shock.

The Brigadier has sent a complimentary message as to the good work officers and men are doing.

27 August 1916

We are to be relieved tonight and anxiously await the relieving forces. Later, the Colonel and I, after the relief is complete, set off to find our horses in the **Talus Boise**. Raining cats and dogs and in the chalk and clay walking is most difficult. We strike the **Maltzhorn Ravine**. The Colonel is walking at his usual rate, apparently fifty miles an hour and **Hepper** is rushing along behind slipping back one step for every two forward. Why didn't I have longer nails in my boots? It is very dark and the Colonel's voice reaches me from about twenty yards ahead, 'Come along **Hepper**, where are you?' A mournful voice from a shell hole greets him with, 'Coming, Sir' and once more I struggle out of a shell hole, wet to the skin. This is repeated several times during the journey. I never could see like a cat in the dark.

We meet **Bell** and his company in **Casement Trench** and put him on the right track, we then go on alone. The Colonel wants to cut across the old No-Man's-Land but I suggest a better way – I am sorry I did now as it is much longer. Horses are fortunately waiting for us. We mount. The

Colonel is an Indian Cavalry man and I am, well hardly an expert on a charger and so the end of the journey galloping on very slippery ground is nearly as funny as the foot slogging amid the shell holes. However, we arrive at **Happy Valley** and find that **Hardaker** and the **Padre** have made everything as comfortable as possible in our tents.

28 August 1916
Cleaning up at **Happy Valley**. Several officers go down with dysentery.

This place is not far from **Bois Celestines** where we encamped on coming to the **Somme**. It is a treeless, desolated valley between two smooth hills and its name is rather an anachronism.

We read **Philip Gibbs'** account of our last stunts and I append a copy of the *Daily Chronicle* cutting:

THE PETER PANS OF WAR
BANTAMS COURAGE IN ATTACK
FIGHTING IN A HEAT WAVE

By **Philip Gibbs,** *The Daily Chronicle* Special Correspondent with the British Army in the field, July 31

"For two days now the sun has been blazing hot, and our fighting men have been baked brown. It is not good fighting weather for either guns or men. A queer haze is about the fields, as thick at times as a November mist and yet thrilling with heat, so that artillery observation is not good for anything like long-range shooting.

"**Mametz Wood**, which is now well behind the lines, looms up vaguely, and, beyond, **Delville Wood** is hardly visible except as a low-lying smudge on the sky-line. Yet the sun is not shaded by the haze, and strikes down glaringly upon the white roads and the trampled fields, upon transport crawling forward in clouds of dust that rise like the smoke of fires about them, and upon soldiers trudging along with their rifles slung and their packs slipping, their iron helmets thrust forward over their eyes and their faces powdered white as millers'.

HOT WORK
"It is hot and thirsty work, and painful to the spirit and flesh of men, even along roads that are not pebbled with shrapnel bullets. Men on the march today were glad of frequent halts, and fling themselves down on the waysides panting and sweating, moistening their dusty lips with parched tongues and fumbling for their water-bottles. They were lucky

to have water, and knew their luck. It was worse for the men who were fighting yesterday in the same heat wave up by **Waterlot Farm** and further south by **Maltzhorn Farm**, not far from **Guillemont**.

"Some of them drank their water too soon, and there was not a dog's chance of getting any more until nightfall... Thirst, as sharp as redhot needles through the tongue, tortured some of these men of ours.

"And yet they were lucky, too, and knew their luck. There were other men suffering worse than they, the wounded lying in places beyond the quick reach of stretcher-bearers. "It was fair awfu' to hear them crying," said one of their comrades. "It was 'Water! Water! For Christ's sake – water!" till their voice died away.

PITY FOR A FOE

"As usual the stretcher bearers were magnificent and came out under heavy fire to get the men in until some of them fell wounded themselves. And other men crawled down to where their comrades lay and, in spite of their own thirst, gave the last dregs of their water to these stricken men. There were many Sir Philip Sydneys there, not knighted by any accolade except that of charity, very rough fellows in their way of speech, but pitiful.

"There was one of them who lay wounded with some water still in his bottle by his side. Next to him was a wounded German groaning feebly and saying, 'Wasser! Wasser!' The Yorkshire lad knew enough to understand that word of German. He stretched out his flask and said, "Hi, matey, tak a swig o' that." They were two men who had tried to kill each other.

"On one part of the battlefields there were some of the Bantam Battalion, these little game-cocks for whom most of us out here have a warm corner in our hearts, because they are the smallest fighting men in the British Army, and the sturdiest, pluckiest little men one can meet on a long day's march. They have been under fire in several parts of this line, where it is not good for any men except for duty's sake.

"It has generally been their fate to act in support of other troops whom it is an honour to support when they go into action because their regiment won fame on the battlefields of Europe since the Napoleonic Wars.

"But it is always a dangerous honour to be in support. The attacking troops have often an easier time than those who lie behind them with scanty cover. It is here that the enemy's barrage is likely to fall and there is not much life being under shell-fire hour after hour perhaps for two days without seeing the enemy or getting at him. The ground becomes covered with dead and wounded.

"The Bantams hold on in hours like this, held on gamely and with wonderful grit. They became great diggers, and because they are not very high, a shallow trench was good enough for cover, and they burrow like ants. "They would as soon forget their rifles as their shovels," said one of their officers today. "There is no need to tell them to dig. They get to work mighty quick, being old soldiers now who have learnt by experience."

MIDDLE-AGED BANTAMS

"They are old soldiers in cunning and knowledge, but there are young lads among them. Old and young (and there are many middle-aged Bantams who stand no higher than 5ft. in their socks) they are all the Peter Pans of the British Army – the-Boys-who-wouldn't-grow-up, and like the heroic Peter Pan himself, who was surely the first of the Bantams, they are eager for single combat with the greatest enemy of England, Home and Beauty who may come along. They had their chance yesterday, and brought back a number of enormous Bavarians as prisoners fairly captured.

"A certain Bantam, ex-boiler maker of Leeds ("the grandest city in the world," he says), and the King's Jester of the battalion, was enormously amused by the incident. He said each Bantam looked no higher than the match-stick to the candle with each Bavarian. To all these little men the German soldiers looked like giants, but like so many Hop-o'-my-thumbs they took charge of these Bavarian Blunderbores and brought them back in triumph. They went searching for them in the ruins of a village some days ago, and found some of them sniping from the trees. They brought them down with a crash, and collected souvenirs.

"This village was a dreadful place when some of the Bantams went into it. Only a few ruins remained, and about these many soldiers of many different regiments went prowling in search of Germans who were still concealed in dug-outs and shell-craters, and who still defended the outskirts of the village with machine-guns, which swept the streets.

"There were Highlanders there, so 'fey' after their fierce fighting that they went about with their bayonets, prodding imaginary Germans, and searching empty dug-outs as though the enemy were crowded there. The ground was strewn with dead, and from ruined trenches and piles of broken bricks there came cries of wounded men. There were many wounded – Germans as well as British – and our men tended them with a heroic self-sacrifice which is described with reverence and enthusiasm by many officers and men. It was a chaplain attached to the South Africans who fought so desperately and so splendidly in 'Devil's Wood'. This 'padre' came up to a dressing station established in the one ruin which could be used for shelter and applied himself to the wounded with a spiritual devotion that was utterly fearless.

"In order to get water for them, and the means of making tea he was in a danger spot marked down by German snipers, who shot our men agonising with thirst, as though they were tigers going down to drink. They are justified according to the laws of war, but it was a cruel business. There was one German officer there, in a shell hole, not far from the well, who sat with his revolver handy to pick off any man who ventured to the well, and he was shot dead.

CHAPLAIN'S COURAGE

"But he did not shoot the padre. Something in the fine figure of that chaplain, his disregard of all the bullets snapping about him, the tireless, fearless way in which he crossed a street of death in order to help the wounded, held back the trigger-finger of the German officer, and let him pass. He passed many times, untouched by bullets or machine-gun fire, and he went into its worst places, which were pits of horror, carrying the tea, which he had made from the well-water, for men in agony, because of their wounds and thirst.

"They were officers of the Bantams who told me the story, though the padre was not there, and their generous praise was good to hear. It was good also to hear the talk of these men who had just come out of battle with the grime and dirt of war upon them, about the men they love to command.

"These young officers are keen, bright-eyed fellows, and in spite of all they had been through – things not yet described – they bore but little trace of their endurance. I sat with them under a tent propped up by stretcher-poles, with the flap tied to an old cart, while men who had just marched down were lying in groups on the field mostly without shirts because of the heat and the long time since they had changed their clothes.

PETER PANS OF WAR

"Afterwards I went among the men – all Peter Pans – who came from all parts of Scotland and the North of England, so that their speech is not easy to a man from the south. They were talking of German snipers and German shells, of all they had suffered and done, and the boiler-maker, their comic turn, was egged on to say outrageous things which caused roars of laughter from the Bantam crowd. The language of the boiler-maker on the subject of Germans and the pleasures of war would be quite unwritable, but the gist of it was full of virtue and suited the philosophy of these five-foot Coeurs-de-Lion, who were grinning round him.

"It is the philosophy of our modern knights, who take more risks in one day than their forebears in a lifetime, and find grim and sinister humour in the worst things of war."

29 August 1916

I go forward with a billeting party to meet the other parties of our brigade at 10.30am so am on the main **Albert Road.**

2pm still here, the lorries have not yet turned up. At last we are off. Much bad language has been caused in fitting the Lewis gun carriers in the lorries, this was not improved by our long wait. We have to unpack at the supply column later on to meet some new lorries which we are to take on. Someone has bungled. No lorries have been ordered and **the A.S.C. [**Army Service Corps**] Captain** in charge of the camp will not let us take our own lorries on. I don't know his name but I have never met a more objectionable person. We are not invited into the mess but remain in the rain until 6.30pm when we pack up again on receiving orders from Division.

Our journey takes us through **Amiens** which is being hidden in the falling darkness. **Canaples** is reached about 12.30pm and at 1.15am we arrive in **Antheux** and wake **Ross** who has gone to bed and almost given us up. The **West Yorkshires** and **Royal Scots** are to billet in **Bernaville.** The narrow road to that place is muddy and twice does the motor lorry stick in the mud and the wheels have to be roped round to obtain a grip. At 3am we wake up the hotel keeper at the village and as there are no beds ready, we sleep in chairs in the kitchen. In the morning omelettes are prepared for us and then we start billeting.

The Battalion is in. Everyone satisfied. Praise be to Allah.

31 August 1916

The billeting party this time on bicycles sets [off] for **Sus St Leger**, the route being extremely pretty.

The old town of **Doullens** set in a valley amid rolling hills calls for a stop and as the day is very hot, we spend an enjoyable hour. I meet **Norman** and have coffee at his hotel. The rest has done us good and we proceed.

The district round **Lucheux** and **Sus St Leger** is fine. The old village of **Lucheux** is situated on the side of a hill surrounded by beautiful woods and far up this the old Chateau or Castle looks out over the expanse of trees.

Having now fixed up billets, we meet the Battalion in the afternoon. **Euselene**, the Brigade Interpreter, comes to my relief at a big house in which I want to secure a headquarters mess. This is the only time I have been really stuck, if I can't get this place there is none other available for the C.O. and his august staff.

1 September 1916
Rest. I admire the Padre's Begonias. I live with him.

2 September 1916
Off again to **Hauteville** which, as its name implies, stands on a hill and from which I get my first peep at **Arras,** just in front of which we are to go into line.

3 September 1916
I go into **Avesnes-le-Comte** with **Banks**, have tea and make a few purchases at E.F. Canteen. [Expeditionary Force's]

4 September 1916
The C.O. has minutely inspected us on the field by the Divisional School. My snipers pass muster.

5 September 1916
We march to **Duisans.** The Divisional Headquarters has taken all the billets. I am messing pro tem with Z Company.

6 September 1916
Training preparatory to trench warfare again.

7 September 1916
The C.O., Company Commander and I look round the front line preparatory to taking over.

8 September 1916
Preparing to go into the trenches tomorrow.

9 September, 1916
We march to **Arras**. I have arranged billets in the street called Les Trois Visages. The men are billeted in the archives of the Museum.

10 September 1916
We are parading to take over. The route is via **Lille road**, **St Nicholas** and **Sunday Avenue** which has its commencement at St Nicholas Church. **Sunday Avenue** is a long communication trench.

11 September 1916
I am busy getting my sniper posts in order and am picking out principal

The village of Thelus, seen here before the war, was fortified by the Germans, but the houses became a heap of ruins. See diary entry below..

features of the landscape behind Boche lines.

The German fortified village of **Thelus** can be seen on the left. It is now a heap of ruins with the exception of a few whitewashed houses. Further to the right up the hill stretches the large wood which hides the villages of **Farbus/Farber** and **Willerval**. The hill there dips down into the valley of the scarp above which towers the village of **Mondry** commanding views, very wide, of our own back areas.

12 September 1916

I am on the scent of a German sentry whom I can see from my observation post and we wish to put in a sniper loophole nearer to him if we can find the exact location which is difficult to fix from my distant O.P. in **Sunday Avenue**. I go with **Martin** into the **Kiek crater** lip. We are looking through the periscope, which the enemy has apparently spotted when we were interrupted by a rifle grenade bursting in the parapet less than a yard from us. **Martin** is hit and his eyes filled with dirt. I receive my quota and I think I ought to be hit but am not. We retire gracefully under a shelter whilst a few more grenades are sent over. I tend **Martin's** wound and find that a piece of grenade has penetrated and remained in his cigarette case, not touching him. I have often heard of this kind of luck but have not seen it before. **Martin** goes to hospital on account of his injured eye.

13 September 1916

The Cheshires carry out a raid or try to but have not much success. We come up for our share of retaliation.

14 September 1916

I have a little dugout in earthwork[?] with **Thurgood; Sergeants Dye** and **Robinson** are in a small shelter above us. We style it Ciros.

15 September 1916

A small patrol of ours is bombed by our own men while coming in. **Private Millar** is killed.

16 September 1916

We are relieved by the 17th Royal Scots. I take over command of W. Company during the absence on leave of **Captain Rose.** Having always been in a specialist job, company work seems strange.

We go into **Roclincourt,** I am OC **Roclincourt** Defences. The men are not at all comfortable as the large dugout on **Wednesday Avenue**, generally used by the troops, is unfit and so the remaining men have to sleep in the open trench. **Banks** is messing with us as he is the Support Company to the people in the line.

17 September 1916

General inspection of the post.

18 September 1916

Banks and I go to dinner at the 18 H.L.I. [Highland Light Infantry] whose battalion Headquarters is in **Roclincourt.**

19 September 1916

Roclincourt is a small village about a thousand yards behind our front line. Few houses remain, merely the skeletons – bare whitewashed walls. Of the church only the east end and a wall remains. The French earlier in the year had heavy casualties here and being the key to the valley to the north of **Arras** it is itself a very important defence.

20 September 1916

My men go in relief to **Arras** to bath.

21 September 1916

Preparing to return to trenches tomorrow.

22 September 1916

We take over the left Sector of the right battalion frontage, namely the worst bit of the line in the vicinity of **King** and **Kite Craters**. We march in via **Laurence Avenue**.

A relief is generally rather a slow process, a long file of men fairly heavily equipped, marching slowly by along narrow trenches followed up by the cooks with their camp kettles and the Company Commander. They have to keep closed up in order not to lose their way in the maze of trenches and it is naturally slow going. The word is occasionally passed down from the front, "Are you all closed up?" and is returned by, "All closed up" or, "Slower in front" to enable the gap to be remedied. Here and there a clumsy man falls off the duck board or down a hole and there is a clatter of falling equipment, mess tins and rifle, covered by a few choice words which lexicologists generally leave out of their dictionaries. When the positions have been reached each man is shown his appointed place and the sentries are told off. This being done, the relieved people slowly march away. Occasionally in a badly managed relief two companies may meet, then comes the trouble. One has to stand as much to one side as possible and the other proceeds to squash past, cheerfully or generally the reverse, knocking the muzzles of their rifles against the faces of the incomers in their anxiety to get back to rest and a 'clean up'.

23 September 1916

I show the Colonel round the line. He generally rather hurries round this place, for which I am pleased.

24 September 1916

Shield and **White** arrived yesterday and take over platoons. **Shield** is very keen on wiring and **White** is anxious to go out on patrol with **Lance-Corporal Ward** who is the keenest patroller I have met. He was one of my scouts in England.

25 September 1916

I have been very careful these last few days as **Rose** comes back today and I go on leave tomorrow. The Boche has been rather a nuisance with his trench mortar blowing in the trench in several places.

I am not going to tempt Providence.

Our Company Headquarter's dugout has been fairly well taped down and the lights have been repeatedly blown out by concussion.

Cheers, **Rose** has arrived and taken over.

A typical tree-lined road in northern France, here with black poplar, Populus nigra, *hybrids; aspens,* Populus tremula, *are also planted.*

26 September 1916

Thurgood and I, packs on our back are hurrying down the communication trench, **Sunday Avenue** as fast as our legs can carry us. We are going on leave. The first time for nine months and we are anxious to get out of the danger zone and no wonder.

We are sitting on a heap of road metalling, resting after our three mile walk from **Arras.** Once more we set off for **Duisans** along the main **Arras** road flanked by a row of poplars. Why do all French roads have an avenue of poplars? I understand that Napoleon constructed straight military roads and as the poplar was a favourite tree of his, these avenues were planted in consideration of him.

We take the mess cart from **Duisans,** our transport lines, to **Aubigny** where we entrain.

We arrive at **Boulogne** about 9.30pm and as the hotels are full we are advised to apply for private rooms at the Notary Herbert's, 93 Rue des Villiards, near the English church. We repair there and have a very comfortable room and a good meal.

27 Sept. 1916

After an excellent breakfast, we catch the boat for England.

LEAVE IN LEEDS, 28 September to 7 October 1916
Of the good time I had there I need not write, and it passes away only too
quickly.

RETURN TO ARRAS AND THE SOMME
8 October 1916
I return to France and spend the night at the Louvre Hotel **[Boulogne].**

9 October 1916
I arrive at **Duisans** and stay with **Hardaker** and learn from him that the
D.L.I. [Durham Light Infantry] are setting off gas tonight and that a mine is
going to be blown.

   Glad we decided to stay down. We have had gas installed for some period and had hoped it had been got rid of during our leave. However, if they
get it away tonight so much the better.

10 October 1916
We go to the trenches (**Thurgood** has come back with me) and I take over
from **Fry** who has temporarily had my job.

12 October 1916
The D.L.I. and Canadians, on my left, send off their gas. There is a pretty
big bombardment. Our artillery was firing rather short and killed a few men
in **Katie Crater.**

13 October 1916
Houston has just come up and asked if I would take his place at Brigade
while he is away. This is the third time I have been asked, so think that a
fortnight's Brigade work will give me an insight into the work. The C.O.
rather demure saying that he is short of officers and that he was going to let
me do company duty. He, however, relents and I go and take over.

13 to 25 October 1916
The work 13 to 25 October, when **Houston** arrives back has been most
interesting. **Major Willis**, our new Brigade Major, joined the same day as
I did and we get on well together. I know the line and he doesn't so we confer together over maps. Most of my time is spent in drawing maps, entering aeroplane photographs, and in walking up to the line each day to see the
observation posts. I have had my gramophone all the time and we play it
when we have time. It is much appreciated .

26 October 1916

Houston has arrived back and I have handed over and return to the battalion. **Major Willis** has thanked me for the trouble I have taken.

I take over command of Z Company while **Rutherford** goes on leave.

27 October 1916

I parade the men of the Company and tell them that though they are resting there is a great deal of work to be done in the trenches and that it is essential to have the mud and water cleared away. Large working parties are sent out.

28 October 1916

I am told by the Colonel that the General wants me to go back permanently as Brigade Intelligence Officer in **Houston's** place. I feel a beast but am advised to take it.

29 October 1916

I hand over Z Company to **Jenkinson** and return to Brigade and take up my new duties which are much more interesting than anything I have yet had.

I have an excellent bedroom and our Brigade Headquarters is in the house of a soap manufacturer in Rue St Augustine near Rue Pasteur [Arras]. What a lovely place **Arras** has been. Its narrow cobbled streets, its rows of little ancient and carved stone houses, one of which **Robespierre**

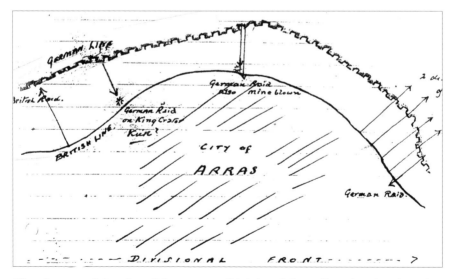

Sketch map of the city of Arras area Divisional front line showing location of British and German raids in November 1916.

Arras showing the splendid Hotel de Ville, the Town Hall, before the war.

was born in, and its Grand Place surrounded by staircase gabled Spanish-Flemish arched buildings.

The German front line now runs practically through the mill in the background. A very strong support line is being constructed along the road with poplars on the horizon known as the **Pont du Jour.**

Ecurie also just behind the line near **Roclincourt** is seen on the left of the photograph [not reproduced here].

The Petite Place, in which stands the old **[Arras]** Hotel de Ville, has been pitifully shelled and little remains save a quantity of broken bricks and stones of the lower walls of the once magnificently carved old Town Hall. This is a favourite haunt of German shells and one is advised to hurry quickly through here lest perchance ill may befall him.

Through the cloisters of the Cathedral is the Museum formerly a convent, now merely a skeleton, whose treasures were nearly all destroyed by fire during the early stages of the war.

Notices are posted around the town to the effect that people are only allowed on duty during the day and must keep close to the walls for fear of aeroplane observation. Regulations are very strict and are under the French Commandant.

The billets still contain their furnishings and are exceedingly comfortable. There are still about 800 civilians, mostly old women and Sisters of Mercy, in the city and each week appears to take its toll from this little community, whose "all" is in **Arras** and with it they will remain to the last.

7 GUERRE 1914-1916. —ARRAS. —CE QUI RESTAIT DE L'HÔTEL DE VILLE ET DU BEFFROI APRÈS LE NOUVEAU BOMBARDEMENT DU 21 OCTOBRE. LE BEFFROI FRAPPÉ PAR UN DERNIER OBUS S'EFFONDRE SUR LUI-MÊME À 11 H. 12. — WHAT REMAINS OF THE TOWN HALL AND THE BELFRY AFTER THE BOMBARDMENT OF THE 21 TH OF OCTOBER. THE TOWER AFTER A LAST OBUS FALLS DOWN. *Visé Paris n 2559*

Arras, the total destruction of the Hotel de Ville, following the bombard-ment in 1916.

At night the shops open for a few hours and in season, nearly every requirement may be bought. The streets suddenly spring to life; there seem to be thousands of people and all the transport wagons arrive, artillery ammunition wagons and civilian produce carts under the cover of darkness. No lights are allowed but I believe at the same time it is not quite so dark 1,500 yards behind the Front Line as it is at night in Leeds.

30 October 1916
I visit my observation posts as usual and see **Thurgood** who has taken over the Battalion Observers. **Blower** is very sorry that I have left.

1 November 1916
Call at Z Company on my way round to wish them luck with the raid which they are to do tomorrow night. The raid was to have been tonight but the Cheshires made too much of a diversion and woke the enemy up.

2 and 3 November 1916
Busy as usual with air photos and reports.

The battalion do a raid at night and I append the account as received at the Brigade:

"A raid on the hostile trenches at point G.6c 8.9 was carried out at 1.40am on the 2-3rd November by a party of the 17th West Yorkshire

93

Regiment. The raid was a surprise one, the men being cut off by means of two Bangalore Torpedoes, the placing of which was covered by machine gun fire, which the enemy had been educated up to expect between 1am and 3am by previously traversing his parapet and wire for several nights in succession.

"On the explosion of the Bangalore Torpedoes the assaulting party moved forward, the artillery, 2" T. Ms and Stokes guns opened a box barrage on the C.T.'s and trenches round the point of entry in accordance with the programme. The parties assembled in trench 103 and proceeded to the starting point, several large shells at G 6.c 5.75 about 220 yards from trench 103. About 7pm **Lieuts. Rose** and **Battishill,** one NCO and two men left trench 103 and laid a tape to the starting point. Later when it became darker the two officers advanced to the gap in the wire which had been cut through on the night of 31st of Oct. They cleared the 15 feet which they had cut through and cut another 3ft of wire and found there still remained about 30ft of wire to get through so decided to use [omission] carried up ladders, traverse mats etc. They arrived at the starting point at 11.40pm.

"At 10.30pm **Lieuts. Rutherford** and **Cleghorn** (RE), the torpedo party and three sappers left trench 103 carrying the torpedoes, the long one weighing about 130lbs and the other about 90lbs. They arrived at the starting point about midnight and handed over the torpedoes to **Lieuts. Rose** and **Battishill** who with help of four men began pushing the torpedoes towards the German wire, a distance of about 30 yards. They covered the distance in about 25 minutes and waited for the machine gun to open fire at 12.30am. The machine guns started and the torpedoes were pushed up the gap. **Lieut. Battishill** then crawled under the wire to within 6 yards of the German parapet, pulled the long torpedo up to him and pushed it through. The short one was placed touching the long one, and the whole party returned to the shell holes arriving about 1.30am. The assaulting party, two trail layers, 3 stretcher bearers arrived at the starting point at 1.15am and were placed in position by **Lieut. Rutherford.** Two telephonists laid a wire from the dugout at the junction of **Victoria Street** and the front line to the starting point in No-Man's-Land. The telephone proved very useful and communication was kept up by means of it during the whole operation.

"**Lieut. Cleghorn** exploded the two torpedoes simultaneously at 1.30am, a clear gap 10 to 12 feet wide was cut by the explosion and the assaulting parties lead by **Lieut. Rutherford** and **Rose** had no difficulty in leading their parties into the German trench. **Lieut Rutherford** ran into the right hand sentry who fired at him, his bayonet was not fixed. **Lieut. Rutherford** killed him with three shots from his revolver, pulled off his shoulder straps and advanced down the trench, he met another German

The interior of Arras Cathedral ruined after the bombardment of the city by German artillery. See diary entry for 29 October 1916.

round the first traverse and killed him with two shots, he saw four more who bolted, he ran after these firing his revolver but did not hit them. They ran into the artillery barrage. **Lieut Rutherford** also ran into the artillery barrage and was buried but was pulled out unhurt, he fired ten shots from his revolver.

"Meanwhile the right hand raiding party bombed two dugouts with 'P' bombs. No enemy emerged from them so several mills [bombs] were thrown down. No sounds were heard.

"**Lieut Rutherford** with the left blocking party and raiding parties met no enemy and they proceeded down the trench until stopped by our artillery barrage. Later the raiders found three Germans who probably came out of dugouts, all three were bayonetted by **Cpl Box, Sergt May** and **C.S.M. Wood.** The left raiders bombed three dugouts with 'P' bombs, no enemy emerged so mills were thrown down and no sounds were heard.

"At 1.55am the recall signal was sounded and the whole party returned to starting point by 1.59am. Our casualties were one other rank slightly wounded in the shoulder by shrapnel.

"The enemy's retaliation was very weak, he appears to have fired all his trench mortar ammunition during the afternoon of 2nd instant. The right blocking party **(Lieut Rutherford)** came across a T.M. [omission] … on to the fixed steps, caught hold of the struts and pulled themselves up, the ladders were not used.

"During the operations Very lights were fired continually from **Kent and Katie Craters** over the point of entry. The German trenches were well lighted up and it proved a great help to the assaulting parties.

"Normal conditions were resumed at 2.08am and 32 men entered the German trenches."   (Sd.) **F. St J. Atkinson**
                                        Lieut. Col.
                                        3.11.16 Commdg. 17th W.Yorks. R.

4 November 1916
Very busy with aeroplane photographs and reports as we expect being relieved about the fifteenth and there is always a good deal of work attached to a thorough handing over.

[**5-12 November 1916** no diary entries]

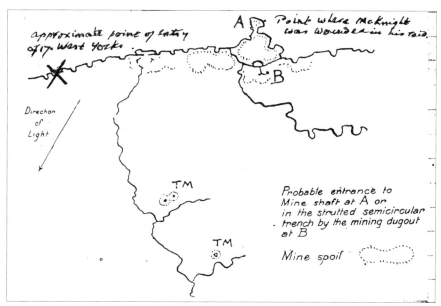

Sketch map of German trenches (called the Pope's Nose) drawn from an aerial photograph. See diary entry for 13 November 1916.

13 November 1916

The Germans have bombarded **Gridiron Line** with trench mortars and blown up an O.P.

The other night **McKnight** and a few other Royal Scots attempted a surprise raid on the **Popes Nose**, it was unsuccessful. **McKnight** and another officer were wounded.

Aeroplane photograph [see page 96] showing the approximate entry of raiders, also the "Popes Nose" Peninsular in the German Front System.

14 to 24 November 1916

I go up several evenings to prepare a dummy work to draw the enemy's fire. Four shells arrive at … [omission in copy].

25 November 1916

A fresh report comes in that the gas is going over at 1.45pm [am] and another at 2.30am or thereabouts. The time for the raid is nearing. Zero hour is 2am. 1.45am gas goes over further south at 2am. A mine goes up on the 105th front and a German raiding party enters the trenches of the Cheshires who take two prisoners, a whole one and a half one. At the same time a large raid is made on the Lancashire Fusiliers who unfortunately, we hear later, lose about 26 men who were captured in a dugout.

Our Brigade Sector is not left untouched and a party of the enemy after a heavy bombardment enter **King Crater** and pounce upon poor **Mundy** of the D.L.I. [Durham Light Infantry] who is doing duty. He throws his mace at them and they fly thinking it is a bomb. In retiring they throw a bomb catching **Mundy** in the legs, killing him. A little further down another officer is killed.

This has spoilt the Durham's own raid as it is timed for the same hour. The artillery having a good deal to do, being also occupied with the Boche raid at **King Crater**, fall short and into the D.L.I. raiding party. An officer and a few men enter the trenches and a number of men terrified by their own shells bursting among them return to their own lines. A dugout is bombed but no Germans are seen. Truly a muddle. The 104 Brigade discharge gas again about 2.30am. Thus on the ... [omission in copy]

26 November 1916

I go up to the D.L.I. Headquarters to find out what has happened. **Moore**, Brigade Bombing Officer, discovers a bomb in **King Crater** and takes it to pieces at Brigade Headquarters. It is an improvised German one for blowing up dugouts and when opened found that the packing contains an identification namely 34 Battalion of Pioneers, No 1 Company.

The remaining companies are at **Ypres,** I believe.

27 November to 1 December 1916
Very busy preparing large maps for handing over, also entering aeroplane photographs. [Omission in copy.] Map and some of the tunnels go beneath the front line.

3 December 1916
We march through **Haute-Avesnes** to **Foufflin-Ricaud [Ricametz?]** a few miles from **St Pol.** We arrive very tired.

4 December 1916
We have our mess in a little cottage. My bedroom is in a large house opposite the Maire's House. This is quite a small village with no shops and will just hold the Brigade Headquarters, the French Mortar Battery and the Machine Gun Corps.

5 December 1916
I am arranging a Brigade Observation and Sniper School as I understand we are here some time. I go over to the HLI and ask for some volunteers for sniping and appear to have some good men. The class is to assemble on 17th.

6 December 1916
Hunt up a range and make targets. I have applied for **Blower** to help me in the work.

7 to 22 December 1916
I think this is the most enjoyable time I have had in France. My Sniping Class of about eighteen men have been excellent and we [have] had some good and interesting lectures, talks and marches. The snow fell heavily and we have been able to conceal tracks. At the end of the course everyone said how sorry they were to go back to their battalions and they all want to be Brigade Observers. I felt very flattered. We have some good shooting.

19 December 1916
The staff have gone to see the Battalions at **Arras** in order to discard a number of injured men who have come up in drafts. They are to be inspected by **Gen. Haldane.**
   Similar inspections have taken place here and some excellent drafts have

Captain Hepper, seated in the front row, third from left.

been sent to the H.L.I. [Highland Light Infantry] and Royal Scots. My servant is marked P/B Permanent Base and I am sorry to say will have to leave me.

I don't know whether I have described old **Harris**. He came to me at Skipton [West Yorkshire] and has been with me ever since. A little bird-like man about 5ft high, he is an excellent servant and absolutely 'mothers [?]'.

He hates the army and all that appertains to it but is I believe very fond of me. He has a little habit of choking his other officers off, which is rather a bad habit to acquire in the army and has several times led him into hot water. **Harris** and I are great 'Pals' and I have never fallen out with him. I shall be sorry to lose him.

25 December 1916, Christmas Day
It may seem strange but this is the first Christmas I have spent away from home. As we are out of the line, we have a holiday and a good dinner at night with an excellent turkey which cost us 55 francs. We drink the health of the King [George V] and then absent friends. I recite at a French Mortar Battery Concert after dinner.

26 December 1916
I apply for leave as we are to be out at least another month and it is a good opportunity to get it.

28 December 1916

I am told by the Colonel that he has been over to tell me that I am to go on leave on the eighth of January.

30 December 1916

The General informs me that **Eadie** and I are to mess with the French Mortar Battery, as, by a Divisional Order, we are to have an R.E. Officer attached for village improvement. We joined the T.M.B. Mess this morning. **Martin** is in charge as **Braithwaite** and **Kelly** and nearly all the battery are at **Liguy Schloss** a few miles away.

31 December 1916 to 8 January 1917

I can hardly possess my soul in patience until January 8th.

8 January 1917

I go on leave with **DeLissa,** who is going to the bath and find that **Eadie** and **McPake** are also going on leave.

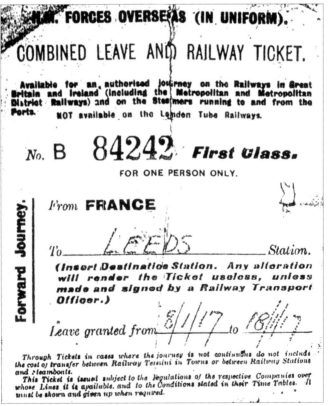

Travel permit for leave in England.

LEAVE IN LEEDS, 8-18 January 1917

RETURN TO THE SOMME BATTLEFIELD
19 January 1917
I arrive back at brigade and find they have moved into a smaller room and so I am instructed to rejoin my battalion for the time being and move with them to rejoin the brigade for duty whenever we go into the line, as there is little to do when out of the line unless a sniping class is in progress and under the circumstances this is not convenient.

I mess with X Company and take over the snipers while **White** becomes Battalion Musketry Officer. **De Witt,** our old Bombing Officer, has come back again and so we are going to have a No. 2 Mess when we get to a better village. This is very small and no suitable mess can be found.

6 February 1917
Our holiday, or so we may call it, appears to have come to an end and we hear that we are going down to the **Somme Area** again. How awful, we had enough of that last year.

I am picked up by **Ross** in an ambulance and go billeting; old interpreter **Boullin** and NCOs follow on bicycles. I am dropped at **Fortel,** complete the billeting and have an omelette. The battalion arrives here at about two thirty and appears to be satisfied with its billets.

Col. Atkinson left when I was on leave and our new colonel arrived yesterday. I have just met him and he seems very nice: **Lieut.-Col. Drew** Northamtonshire Regt. He always wears a starched linen collar and a cigarette holder.

7 February 1917
Ross again picks me up in the ambulance about three miles out of **Fortel** and we make for **Rebreuve Chateau** which is to be Brigade H.Q. We go then on to **Outrebois,** and **Boullin** and I billet. I understand from Town Major that we can have the whole of the village but discover just before the battalion comes in that only half the village belongs to us and we are to commence again. It is going to be a terrible squash, and I have hardly any officers' billets or messes when the battalion arrives. I manage to get everyone settled in time. We get to No 2 mess. **DeWitt, White, Thurgood** and myself. **Outrebois** is not far from **Doullens**, nestling in a valley.

8 February 1917
The old ambulance is having a good run these last few days, and it again awaits me and we proceed to **Havernas**; I am dropped here while the oth-

ers proceed to billet the remainder of the brigade at **Vignacourt** three miles away.

I think the day has been the king of all days for billeting. The finding of billets has its good points namely the improvement of French, the obtaining of a good billet for the Billeting Officer who, like a good carver, should give all the others the best billets yet keep a good one for himself, and the missing of a long march by either riding cycles or motoring, but it has its bad points.

Having been escorted round the billets by the Deputy Maire (a high-flown title for a shepherd) I have fixed everything up except Z Company and shall finish in about half an hour. **Ross** cruises along saying 'jump in', we are not stopping here after all but are going on to **Yzeux** on the **River Somme** some seven miles away. I instruct my NCOs to follow on their cycles and we again billet and find we can only get half the battalion in as most of the barns are now being filled with corn and beans prior to threshing. **Boullin** and I fix up a splendid place in the Chateau for the CO. I am afraid that all our HQ messes in the Army do not comprise Gentlemen as the M'mselle asks the interpreter in French, believing that I do not speak it, if we are 'drunkards'.

I feel very annoyed but of course do not show that I understand her and I am somewhat flattered to hear the interpreter reassure her in French, 'They are perfect Gentlemen, M'mselle.'

Wilson, AWE to **General Landon,** comes along in a car saying that the remaining two companies are to be fixed up at **Picquiny,** three miles away up the **Somme.** I am taken there, the two NCOs following on cycles. The companies are expected in at 5.30pm and after billeting I wait about, taking turns with the MQs. It is now eight o'clock and pitch dark except for the few streaks of light that escape through the shutters of the windows of the little shops in the main street. I am very annoyed that they don't come as I have some splendid billets for them. Half an hour later **Wilson** arrives in the car saying that the Battalion is remaining, after all, at **Havernas;** so two other officers have had to re-billet in that village as I was away and they didn't know the ones I had selected. It is most annoying to have billeted in three villages today for no purpose. I am dead tired. I have told the NCOs to stay in **Picquiny** for the night and return to Battalion in the morning.

9 February 1917

The Headquarters are staying at the Chateau of **Monsieur le Comte d'Havernas,** an elderly but poor member of an old family. The Comte is in Paris and the Countess and children are living in the Chateau.

My snipers and observers have a good place above the stables. We have an excellent No 2 Mess but the women are rather disagreeable.

10 February 1917

I call on the Companies and take the snipers to the range. This is a charming village, rendered the more so from the fact that we were told it was very bad. The country around on the north side is very hilly with bleak moorland grass; here and there snuggling in some sheltered nook is a white chateau. On the south side, the wide expanse of arable land rolls towards the **Somme** and dips suddenly so that no view can be obtained of that pretty river.

11 February 1917

I have a splendid range and interest my men either in the morning or afternoon by firing from cover at figureheads hidden in bushes and on the side of the hill.

13 February 1917

We hold a concert in a hut on the village square. **Major Hall,** who has returned to us as Second in Command (he left us on the **Somme** to command the Cheshires) organises the show which is attended by the Countess, the heir, and her little daughters. I recite 'The Wedding Speeches'. It has been a splendid concert.

17 February 1917

DeWitt, Thurgood, White and I go to **Vignacourt** to be photographed. We hump a pack containing our 'woolly bears' and tin hats on our heads. The operation is over, we smiled and looked pleasant and have apparently been logged up for a North Pole Expedition. We trust the photograph will be a success. I hate being photographed and think I shall turn a Mohammedan or whatever Sect it is which has to turn the head away when being taken; it is much more becoming.

MOVE TO FRENCH SECTOR, near Rosières
19 February 1917

We learn that we are taking over a piece of the French line in a few days. I go to **Marcelcave** and again billet.

The French people are very nice and as they have seen very few English troops, they are inquisitive and turn out to watch us. We have a very good but cheap lunch in a French cottage. They do not know how to charge yet, fortunately. We find a No 2 Mess in a clean cottage kept by a widow who

'DeWitt, Thurgood, White and I go to Vignacourt to be photographed' on 17 Feb. 1917. Raymond, top right, wearing a sheepskin (print from microfilm).

makes things very comfortable for us.

A French 75 battery has just passed through, followed by a number of small carts carrying Pom Poms and French Mortars. Both English and French are interested in one another.

22 February 1917
I ride over to **Caix** and billet. This village is about five miles or less from the Line and has only occasionally been shelled. The church tower is very old, massive and quaint with small turrets. **Ross**, who is an architect, tells me this is Renaissance work. The priest has had a bomb on his house and I find him living in one room next to his gardener's cottage.

23 February 1917
We see some of the French troops, which our present battalion have relieved, dragging themselves along. They are stragglers and seem to be coming along at their own sweet time, hours behind the regiment. Their blue uniforms, equipment and unshaven faces are coated with yellow mud and they are fatigued. They were relieved yesterday by the 104th Brigade. This does not auger well for our having a clean time.

24 February 1917

As the Divisional Troops are coming into **Caix,** we are to move into the **Camps des Ballons** which as its name implies used to shelter some French observation balloons. Accommodation is very bad.

25 February 1917

We stroll down to the village and make our purchases of tinned delicacies and French goods. As there are some rather pretty girls in the shop, we improve our French, stay a little longer and make more purchases than we probably should otherwise have done.

26 February 1917

I rejoin the Brigade at **Rosières** which is about two and a half to three miles from the Line and has not been shelled to any great extent, though there are practically no windows with glass in them and the village has been totally evacuated by civilians who have removed all their furniture with the exception of a few tables and chairs in the various Headquarters messes.

We are billeted in a house which has formerly also been a military warehouse. Our offices are in this and our mess and sleeping rooms are in the house apartments.

Rosières consists of about three mean streets and the church, an ugly yellow stone and brick building the tower of which may be seen for some miles. East of the village, the flat country stretches towards our line. The German line just below ours does not obtain a view of the village which is under observation only from Boche balloons. A mile further south is a large sugar factory, the chimney of which can be seen by the enemy and has been the mark[?] of German guns. I understand that fifty shells were aimed at it one day and five direct hits were scored. None of these succeeded in bringing the chimney down though it appears to be somewhat unsafe.

27 February 1917

I go up the line on my pony. Have I introduced you to the "Little'un"? A black mare of about 14 hands, with white star, shaggy mane and pretty tail, well fed and groomed, groggy forelegs and quiet disposition, she has probably been a lady's pony at some time and I know that I am fairly safe while riding as she doesn't kick, doesn't bite, doesn't run away, doesn't exert herself; in fact doesn't do anything that is supposed to make riding the best sport in the world. The "Little'un" has only three speeds, slow – damn slow – and stop. She is however much pleasanter than one I had in England, which always did want to go the way you didn't and went too sometimes.

28 February 1917

Our present Brigade Front runs just west of the Chateau of **Chaulnes**, which overlooks our line and is at times decidedly unpleasant on account of sniping, down to **Bois Broussig**. The actual front line is evacuated on account of mud in several places.

1 March 1917

I have just been up to see **Hadow** but did not find him in. The mud is terrible, up to the waist in place and it behoves one to walk very carefully.

My servant is behind and we struggle through the slough and arrive back at **Lihons,** where our horses are standing, mount after scraping off a little mud and arrive at home thoroughly tired, dirty and very hungry.

2 March 1917

I am busy preparing maps of the line. The men of my battalion are returning to the line very fatigued and are being relieved by the 19 D.L.I.

3 March 1917

During the night the 16th Cheshires lost some prisoners and a machine gun in a German raid on **Bois Frederic** on our right.

4 and 5 March 1917

Up the line as usual.

6 to 14 March 1917

What a great deal can happen in a few days.
1. Poor old **Rose** of W Company was killed by a trench mortar shell and I attended his funeral in **Rosières** cemetery.
2. The Germans made a raid on one of our machine gun posts capturing the gun and leaving a wounded prisoner. The prisoner died on the way down to **Rosières** and I had to go into the mortuary to search him for any papers that might be concealed in his clothing. This was a gruesome business and I was pleased to get away. There is a saying that a good Boche is a dead one but I would rather not see either in uniform.

15 March 1917

We are relieved by the 105 Brigade and return to rest at **Caix.** We have a charming little house which holds our mess, the Brigade Major and staff Captain's room. **Euselene, Greig** and I are further down the road.

During the last few days or weeks reports have been coming in from Division of fires being observed behind the German lines, fires that obviously show that the Germans will retreat or they may be under the impression that we are going to attack and are preparing to lay waste the land. Not only from **Arras** to the south of **Roye** do these reports come, but also from east of **Dixmude** [Ypres area]. For months now the Boche have been talking of his **Hindenburg Line**, a line some 25 or 30 miles forward of where we now are, to which he will retire should we press him hard but through which we shall not be able to pass.

16 March 1917

The Brigadier tells us that we must be ready to move quickly at any moment and we prepare all our things, cut down our kit. I am at present making two or three coloured contour maps of the forward country in case of a general move. The first map I do I make the high ground dark brown and the low ground dark green, which of course is the proper method, but his Lordship the **Staff Captain** does not agree and I have to make another. Moral – it is not considered good policy to argue with the Staff.

17 March 1917

We have just come down to breakfast and are informed by the **General** that we are to pack up now and move to **Rosières.**

I am endeavouring to fix up the last of my maps and from the window that faces on to the main road I can watch the cavalry (King Edward's Horse) going up to wait for a show. They are followed by the Corps Cyclists. Great excitement prevails throughout the village. People, many of whom have fled from **Rosières** and from villages now in German hands are clapping their hands and howling down all kinds of French curses, which happily I do not understand, upon 'Les Sales Boches'.

At 6.30pm on this dark night we move up. Limber signal carts and baggage wagons. The French have taken **Roye**, a few miles further south and liberated 700 French civilians who had been brought there so that there would be less mouths to feed.

We arrive in **Rosières** and billet near the church. The General is very pleased as we are now embarking on open warfare, and is walking about in his little cap comforter, whistling and nodding to himself.

In the afternoon at 2 o'clock the 17th W. Yorks (the first in the Division) occupied the German Front Line meeting no one. Two hours before this the Germans had been sniping heavily from **Chaulnes Chateau**, yet two hours later not a soul remained, nor had anyone seen them go. At night **White, Rose, Jenkins**, and other officers did some good patrols penetrating two and a half miles into the German defences and not observing a single German.

18 March 1917

The 106th Brigade is in Divisional Reserve and the 105th and 104th Brigades extend and take over the ground west of **Omiécourt** and south west of **Hallencourt**. Eventually pushing on further with the 61st Division on the left and 22nd Division on the right.

Our Brigade H.Q. move to **Maricourt [Maucourt],** a village originally a mile behind the recent evacuated front line and in the old front line which was taken by the French in the Somme Push last year. We are in a French Battalion dugout, very strongly built and quite comfortable.

19 March 1917

The Cavalry have gone forward and we hear of local encounters with retreating Germans. I make another contour map.

20 March 1917

I am instructed to report on the railway remaining just behind the front line of the enemy from the **Hallu – Chilly** road to **Chaulnes – Omiécourt** road, a distance of about three miles. I have never made a report on a railway before but with my little book of notes, set out with **Rodley,** my servant. The rails have been electrically fixed at gaps of ten to twenty yards apart thus new lines will have to be relaid entirely. The ballast is little damaged and the shells do not penetrate far into the shingle before bursting. I am rather doubtful as to how long a ruined bridge could be cleared and a temporary one erected but put it down as two days. 1,500 new sleepers only are required in this sector. We came back across the old No-Man's-Land and look back at our old lines from the Boche point of view. I firmly believe that he must have been just as afraid of us as we of him.

21 March 1917 onwards

Col. Newman, G.S.D. Division congratulates me on my railway report. I am elated. During the next few days my battalion is billeted at **Hallu** and I make excursions to see them and to find objects of interest in the German lines and dugouts. One has to be extremely careful as all manner of devices are arranged to blow an unwary Britisher up. Live bombs are placed in the side of dugout entrances, with a hand rail attached; when the rail is pulled by the hand of the person entering, the dugout is blown up.

Bombs are laid under helmets which are likely to be picked up as souvenirs. Boxes when open explode, and dozens of other little playthings of the Boche dog the footsteps of the unwary.

Several old women and other civilians have been up to see what remains of their houses in **Chilly** or the adjoining village of **Maucourt.** It is pathet-

Captain Raymond Hepper, centre, with unknown colleagues in France.

ic to see the old white-haired French woman returning in her country cart weeping 'we cannot find where our home has been.' They had in many cases buried their treasures in the garden before they came away in 1914 but now everything is so altered, trees and landmarks destroyed, houses merely heaps of stones or bricks with just a jagged wall standing here and there, roofing timber strewn about so that even the roads are obscured. Only one case do I know of within the vicinity of these villages, of the treasure being discovered and this was several thousand francs buried only three feet from a German latrine trench. I have often pictured the smile on the faces of those Germans if they had only dug that trench three feet more to the right.

I have scoured the country on my little pony, been to the villages of **Curchy, Puisieurs [Puzeaux], Omiécourt** and **Punchy**. At **Punchy** we came across some concealed machine gun emplacements. On the first sight they appear to be just manhole covers but on entering a dugout and turning a lever the manhole cover rises and the machine gun and crew come to the ground level in position for firing. The **Bois du Hallu** is full of 'pill boxes'. The name of pill box generally used in the **Ypres Sector** is not generally used down here and we give them the correct term of machine gun emplacement or mebus(?). They are constructed of concrete twelve to fifteen feet high and one of these has an iron bridge like a ship, which had probably been used as an artillery O.P. [observation post]. On this and several other prominent places was chalked up 'Gott strafe England.' A good view of our line in front of **Chilly** could be obtained. The wood as a whole was a 'machine gun nest.'

The Division having been cut out of the actual advance pro tem owing to the wiping out of the salient, sets to work to clear and make roads for the guns and ration carts. We return to **Rosières** as the H.L.I. are working on the railway in the vicinity.

I try another horse from the mobile veterinary section and arrange with the sergeant in charge to change it for my little one. The next day I find that the artillery have taken it with the permission of the Division.

Captain Rycroft MC Blackwatch, has taken over Brigade Major from **Ross** who has been acting in the place of **Major Willis** who has just left.

I ride out with **Rycroft** to **Curchy** and district to examine the defences on the **Somme** which we are to complete in case the Boche tries to advance again to either harry us or cut us up.

My horse which I have borrowed from the mobile people has just thrown me. We were just crossing a narrow ditch when he kicked out and over I went into the mud. When I looked back the horse was careering home and was eventually caught by **Bell's groom** about half a mile away.

We move to **Marchlepot** which is rather north of where we were at **Hallu**. The day is frightfully wet and the only billets available are a big German dugout and two tumbledown houses for the accommodation of officers. There is much 'wind up' about the running of German dugouts and the General, Brigade Major and Staff Captain will not sleep in it. **Allan** and I (**Allan** is assistant Staff Capt.) are the only people who sleep there, while our servants occupy the General's bed in the lower gallery. The dugout does not go up while we are there and from its sinister appearance I should not at all doubt that it will go up sooner or later.

In many cases have dugouts, houses and chateaux been blown up by these delayed action mines. The mine is merely a box a few feet square filled with explosive. A detonator is placed in this, above which is a striker pin and spring held up by a piece of wire which passes through a chamber full of acid. The acid eats through this wire gradually according to the thickness. This releases the striker which hits the detonator causing the charge to explode. The box is buried a few feet under the ground and as no wires pass through the ground it is not discovered even by the most delicate searching. It is only luck that sometimes brings them to light.

From **Marchlepot** we march to **Epénancourt**, a factory on the **River Somme** between **St Christ** and **Pargny**. My battalion is billeted at **Pargny**. Our No. 2 Brigade mess is in a little room under a cement tower and is very comfortable. The Germans have destroyed practically every house which could be used as a billet and we are pleased to have such good cover as this over our heads.

What a glorious part of the country this is! Undulating valley rolling up from the banks of the **Somme** with its beds of rushes and iris. Long R.E. [Royal Engineers] bridges cross the river and the roads east through **Falvy** to the front.

Pargny is about a mile further south and has a large German cemetery and in the centre is a statue in grey marble representing a German knight with a Crusader's shield and armour. The bent square ugly head fills the observer with disgust. The maker's name is a firm in Hamburg. I will say that wherever the Germans have left their cemeteries they have been carefully tended and all have statues or memorials and many are enclosed by stone posts and chains. It is truly a cheering sight to realise that the enemy has lost probably as many men as we ourselves.

Two days later in riding round **Pargny** I discovered that the head of the statue has been knocked off. Some British Tommy has evidently not been able to stand the sight of that square **Hindenburg** head. It is now probably lying at the bottom of the **Somme**. In most of the above mentioned cemeteries the monuments are of slate-coloured stone which has evidently been brought down the **Somme** in barges from some distance.

In a few days we proceed to **Ennemain. Ross** has already been over a few

Yellow flag, 'Iris pseudacorus', drawn by Nigel Hepper.

The basilique of Albert near the Somme battlefield is left but a heap of ruins after the bombardment.

days before to fix up billets and says that we have an excellent mess in a house which still has three remaining downstairs rooms intact, though the roof and upper storeys have fallen away. He is an architect in civilian life and assured us it will be quite safe and waterproof.

The day we arrive at **Ennemain** is pouring with rain and **Ross's** beautiful house is dripping with water. There's one dry place in which the table is placed and the people sitting round the table have to waggle their necks to avoid the drops and hope that it will soon stop raining. The B mess, in which I am, has quite a comfortable stable or loose box for its mess.

I have received a note from **Cohen** saying that he has arrived out again from England. I shall be so pleased to see him again as he has been away from the battalion for a year. I am at West Yorks Y Company mess for dinner and see old **Cohen**, just the same as ever.

Later. We are now going to entertain **Cohen** in our mess (this is two days later). The gramophone is rasping out its familiar tunes and after dinner we have a game of bridge.

The next day the Royal Scots and the West Yorks debauch from **Falvy** to attack **Ennemain** in a brigade manoeuvre.

Péronne is quite a nice ride from here and about eight miles distant. **Euselene** and I have been with the mess cart in advance to purchase mess stores at the canteen. Our route lay through **Athies, Prusle** and **Flamicourt.** It is an ancient town, the scene of many engagements and has been destroyed at least three times during wars. It suffered badly in

1500AD approximately. During the war of the Revolution, during the 1871 Franco-Prussian War and now again in this war and there is very little left beyond the skeletons of the houses to show its former prettiness. We went over the Castle, the prison of Charles the Bloody, saw the old gateways and the Town Hall.

Péronne is bounded on the south and west by the wide **Somme**, on the western bank of which ran our old front line. No civilians remain there. Our next resting place, a few days later, is **Monchy-Lagache,** a distance of about four miles east of **Athies.** We spend one night here having taken over from the Warwicks. In passing I may mention that the H.L.I. found in a cellar in **Athies** the dead naked body of a French girl presumably a victim of German brutality.

The next day we proceed to **Vermand** to reconnoitre the new Brigade Headquarters. We are to take over the line on the following day.

We march to **Cavigny Farm** for one night, taking up our abode at **Vermand** on the next day.

10 April 1917

Our Brigade H.Q. is in the only house left standing in this village with the exception of two or three small cottages which are used by headquarters and quarter master stores of the West Yorks which are billeted here. **Vermand** has been a pretty village on the slope of a hill which is capped by a big tumulus behind which stands our farm out of sight and to a certain extent saved from Fritz's artillery. A cou-

Another view of the town of Albert after the bombardment.

Rycroft and I go out on a daylight patrol. We are fixing the positions for advanced posts and crawl out well in front of existing posts to a wood where we have an excellent view of the German salient at **St Helene**. Loup, **Rycroft's** dog, an Alsace Berger, is with us and I am frightened to death that she will give the show away.

We crawl about in a wood and I lose my revolver and have to crawl back to find it. I am successful.

After spending some time in the wood and encountering no Germans we are just thinking of turning back when whizz bang bang, came two shots on the front part of the copse. Whizz bang bang, two more at the rear of the copse, this is decidedly unpleasant and it looks as if old Boche has spotted us, and are going to force a bracket and possibly get us. We beat a hasty retreat out of the wood, over the open ground to the side of it and over the hill where our front posts are situated. We had one or two other similar incidents during the tour. **Rycroft** is a daring fellow and doesn't care a hang where he goes.

15 April 1917
Round the line with **Rodley** examining O.P.s; **White** has an O.P. on the tumulus just in front of the front line. I do not like the position as it is perfectly obvious and is generally strafed with 4.2s and 'woolly bears'.

16 April 1917
At midnight X Coy., 17 West Yorks, under **Captain Bell** raid the enemy trenches at the **St Helene** salient. The southern party get into the trenches and find them unoccupied whilst the northern party are enfiladed by a machine gun. Result ten missing and eight wounded. No officers were hit. Later, some of the missing men return having rather lost direction. I believe only three or four are unaccounted for.

17 to 22 April 1917
Much the same as usual – aeroplanes, maps and O.P.s. I ride up the line each day.

The Boche 'planes are still active when ours have gone home and at 6.30 each night down comes a balloon. I can't make out what our R.F.C. is doing. I thought patrols were always supposed to be out in front of the C.B.s.

23 April 1917
We are relieved and go back to **Cuvigny Farm** for six days. The farm or what is left of it stands on the main road half way between **Tertry** and

Caulaincourt. We made several alterations such as constructing a mess and a B. Mess.

24 to 29 April 1917

These six days in rest have been most interesting. I have not done very much active work; my work takes place when we are in the line. When out of the line I merely visit various Battalion Intelligence Officers, draw a few maps probably and reconnoitre each sector we are to take over next. I have of course to spend a certain amount of time in the office while the staff are wandering about.

30 April to 12 May 1917

We do not take over our old bit of line in front of **Vermand** but relieve the 1st Brigade in **Masteville** railway cutting. The 104 Brigade are in our old H.Q.

On the day of relief I am sure that there is too much traffic showing and that we shall be shelled sooner or later as an observation balloon is up. We are, during the evening. We have a series of huts in the cutting, the mouth of which almost faces the enemy but is only under observation from the enemy balloon on a clear day. 'Persistent Percy', a German long-range 4.2 high velocity gun has already put a few shells on the back above our heads and on the other side of the cutting. There is rather a 'wind up' and **Rycroft** and the General got under the wall of the embankment which abuts on their room and **Ross** and I do the same in his room. There is a large explosion in the cutting, big pieces of earth, ballast and timber come flying down onto the roof and breaking the walls of the hut which is constructed of tarred paper felting.

The General gives the order to clear, which does not need saying [?] twice and we open the door and to our surprise find that the shell has actually burst one foot away from the door. This sounds an exaggeration, but it is not, one foot from the lip of the crater to the door and four yards away from us, yet not a man was injured nor did we feel a very great concussion probably owing to the force being resisted slightly by the felting of the wall, through which one could easily put a pin. If any spectators had been there they wouldn't have seen our heels for dust and we are well clear of the cutting and behind the railway embankment further on. Another shell fell further down the cutting spurring us to further action and so the glittering staff and retinue were forced to give ground for a hundred yards.

I am intensely amused on reaching our embankment, on finding our fat old cook **McDonald** sitting on his haunches, howling down curses on the Germans who had made him leave his beautiful piece of roast mutton which he was preparing for our dinner. "Why did Ah no breeing it wi me, Sirs? Why did Ah no breeing it wi me, Sir" was his wail, "as nice a piece as iver Ah did see." Poor old **McDonald** your meat is quite safe and after all what is the price of meat with the price of one's life.

McDonald's a character, you know Bainfather's one and only Bill; imagine Bill cut down a bit and widened out. A large tummy and wide trousers, as broad nearly as long, a Balmoral Tam o'shanter stuck at a rakish angle on his head instead of the old cap comforter and you have **McDonald,** of the 17th Royal Scots, our Brigade Mess cook.

Our line now runs from the **River Omignon** to halfway between **Falvy** and **Gricourt**. Owing to the shelling mentioned above we have moved our H.Q.under the railway embankment and the offices are further along the cutting. A dugout has been tunnelled for us to shelter in case of accidents. The General has been much disturbed by the Boche building a chord (?) to their trenches in front of **Gricourt** and **Les Trois Sauvages**. The D.L.I. on relief were instructed to take this but were attacked by the Germans and fell back. Later large patrols are sent forward and the West Yorks are to attack this time and establish posts in the **Trois Sauvages** – **Cepy** road and also in the farm itself. The posts are established and prisoners taken, the main post failing to be taken is that of the **Trois Sauvages**.

13 (?) May 1917

The French interpreter attached to my battalion is an antique dealer in Paris in civil life and he is continually finding souvenirs.

In the woods and neighbouring fields are many Cavalry Regiments: the Bengal Lancers, the Poona Horse, the 17th Lancers, 9th Hodoor's (?) Horse and the Deccan Horse. A walk in this district must be something similar to India, large parties of Indians in fatigue dress are gathering fuel, long thin clean-limbed brown men are bathing in the river, great curved-bearded Sikhs salute one smartly in the roads or give "eye-es ri-et" when with a party, whose handsome features turn quickly towards one in salute.

14 May 1917

Yesterday I went up to the **Deccan Horse** camp to fix up a ground for our sports today. An Indian camp is a strange sight. In the horse lines the Indians were busy grooming their horses, singing to themselves. In some corner a group of men were sitting on their hammocks playing some native game and from the edge of the camp came the sound of a distant chant sounding like the repetition of 'Ah-la-la-ah.' Across the road was the officers' mess in front of which tall smart officers, both British and Indian stroll about. The British and Indian officers do not mess together, the latter being as far as I can make out similar to British warrant officers.

The sports take place and in spite of the rain are a great success. The horse jumping is judged by the officers of the Deccan Horse. **General O'Donnell** our Brigadier, presents the prizes. He tells us that this will be the last time he will have the opportunity of speaking to us again as a whole as he is to be relieved by another brigadier and will probably take on some job in England. I am sorry for the old man and I am really quite fond of him.

15 May 1917
We are to move north on the 19th. And so are preparing for the march.

19 May 1917
I am in charge of the brigade party today as **Allan** is billeting and **Greig** is away in front. The order of march is as follows: Royal Scots, H.L.I., D.L.I., the Brigade's Transport and West Yorks. We meet the West Yorks about a mile further up the road to allow it to join in. We switch to the right before we reach **Estrées** and continue along the long straight road to **Péronne.** Arriving there, we billet in the vicarage, this sounds splendid but as there are [omission in copy] which adjoins has been badly damaged and here and there in the middle of the walls are unexploded shells embedded in the stonework. Some say that they have been placed there by the Germans and have in many cases been fused by them to blow the walls down. I cannot think that is correct as it would mean a great deal of time in preparation and I do not think the game would be 'worth the candle.'

Allan and I are settling in our temporary Brigade Office and are sur-prised by a Brigadier General entering and stating that he has come to take over from **General O'Donnell** - sakes alive - our new brigadier and so soon. **General O'Donnell** comes in from the Survey of our new Line east of **Péronne** and is introduced and for some time they are closeted and hand-ing over. During the evening the old man strolls round the office and gives me some advice, 'Hepper, never get old Laddie.'

20 May 1917
I visit the West Yorks No 2 mess and have a jolly evening.

21 May 1917
We are all up betimes and by 10 o'clock are marching east to **Sorrel le Grand** where we are to encamp for the night. On the way we say 'Goodbye' to **General O'Donnell** who stands at the **Bussu** crossroads and takes his last salute.

Arriving at **Sorrel le Grand,** we find that **Allan** has pitched the camp in the wrong place and the next day there is much swearing as the whole thing has to be moved about half a mile away.

23 May 1917
We move into the Line. The West Yorks take over trenches east of **Villers-Guislain** and the D.L.I. are south of them. Both Battalion Headquarters are in the village, in fact so are the support battalions. We are in the railway embankment east of **Raileau Mill**. It is quite nice but likely to be raided by the Boche. We are going to have a dugout constructed under the embankment so as to be on the safe side.

24 May 1917
I visit all the headquarters in **Villers-Guislain.**

25 May 1917
Up the line. I find it is much easier to walk up than ride as one can cut off a corner. I hear at night that **Moore** has been wounded on patrol. He ran up against a Boche post and tried to get through the wire. The Germans bombed him and shot him but emptying his revolver at them he escaped.

26 May 1917
One of our 'planes was brought down.

27 May 1917
The Boche made a small daylight raid on a small post held by my Regiment. The men apparently relied on bombs instead of using their rifles which is fatal, at least it was in this case as one wounded man was taken away prisoner.

28 May 1917
The D.L.I. and H.L.I. go into the line. The West Yorks being now in support.

29 May 1917
I visit battalions and rig up a jolly good observation post in **Villers-Guislain**; this gives me an excellent view of the **Hindenburg Line**, west of **Le Terrier** also **Lateau Wood, Rues-des-Vignes** and **Chenaux Wood.** Poor old **Hadow** was killed today near the church, by a direct shrapnel burst.

30 May 1917

I have been to **Hadow's** funeral at **Hendicourt** and helped to bear the body to the grave.

2 June 1917

We are relieved and go back to **Templeux la Fosse.** This valley is delightful. The valley of **Templeux** is badly ruined and is nearly surrounded by **Henne** woods and in the valley about a mile away lies **Agicourt**; see map on next page but one [in original MS]. On the hill above this is our Brigade

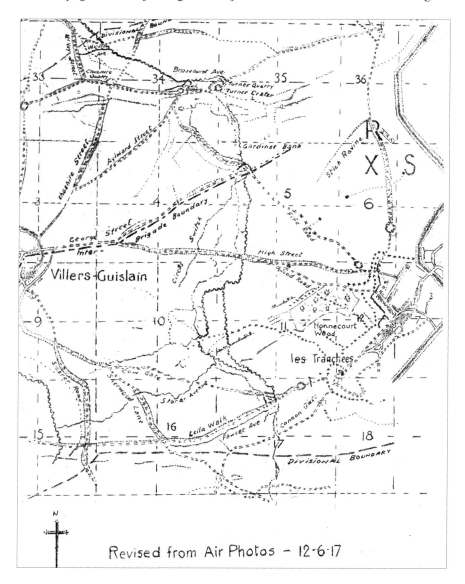

H.Q. camp. The battalion of the brigade are in the valley and looking forward to a few days good rest. The time is filled in by Rifle Meetings, concerts, polo matches and sports.

3 to 23 July 1917
We are in and out of the Line at **Epehy** and **Lempire** south of **Villers-Guislain.**

25 July 1917
The Brigade Headquarters is in an old garden of a once fine house which has been demolished prior to evacuation. Many good observation posts have been established and the following views show the wonderful extent of hostile country which can be seen from the posts.

23 July 1917
Poor old **Cohen** is wounded again.

I hear that **Cohen** is dead. I have lost a true pal**.** Those who read this diary, if any there be, will know how we lived together not only in France but throughout our whole training in England, have known our faults, likes and dislikes and have been true friends. His memory will not fade.

28 July 1917
The Brigade moves to **Longavesnes** where we have manoeuvres. In the heat of a gorgeous day an observation balloon bursts and the occupant jumps out with his parachute which however catches on the basket. It is a pitiful sight to see the man trying to get his knife to cut himself free. Inspite of his struggles he is unsuccessful and sweeps down to his death. An enemy aeroplane is brought down later.

6 August 1917
The Royal Scots are raided in **G(u)illemont Farm**. There is stout resistance by Lewis gunners but some of the garrison are unfortunately captured.

8 August 1917
The West Yorks and D.L.I. relieve the Royal Scots and H.L.I.

11 Aug 1917
The West Yorks are relieved by the 16 Cheshires who are temporarily attached to the brigade while the H.L.I. are on training. I am busy interpreting air photos of the knoll and **G(u)illemont Farm.**

Above, two views of Ramond Hepper's own steel helmet with (now perished) leather inside, see diary entry for 18 March 1916.

Left, a German tobacco pipe ornamented with a picture of Hindenburg (name not shown on this photograph). Raymond Hepper's Great War souvenir, now in the possession of Nigel Hepper.

Cigarette box Christmas present, dated 1914. A metal box, now empty except for a small card dated 1915 and printed in Gothic letters: "With Best Wishes for a Victorious New Year. From The Princess Mary and Friends at Home." As almost everyone smoked at that time, it would have been a very acceptable gift to the troops.

Cavalry caltrop and a metal dart with fearful spikes, both of which were dropped from aircraft onto horses and personnel. Captain Hepper's souvenirs, now in the possession of Nigel Hepper.

Delville Wood in the Somme battlefield, where there is now a memorial to the fallen. In 2008 Nigel Hepper laid a wreath in their memory. See diary entry for 12 July 1916. Photograph by kind permission of Brigadier Johnny Walker.

A Kellog card of a Bristol Fighter aircraft with similar German triplanes behind. Aerial warfare was a new thing in the Great War and Raymond Hepper pioneered interpretation of air photographs of enemy positions. He was attacked by German Gotha bombers near Ypres, see diary entry for 18 October 1917.

BRISTOL F.2.B. FIGHTER

Above Captain E. R. Hepper's World War I and World War II medals.

Pictured left Captain E. R. Hepper's Somme medal.

Below, Private J. V. Heasman's posthumous Great War medals.

12 to 18 August 1917

I am up the Line frequently at the O.P.s etc. and **Rodley** goes up with me as my orderly.

19 August 1917

Assaulting parties of the H.L.I. and the 105th Brigade have been preparing for an attack on the German front line system at the advanced posts in front of **G(u)illemont Farm** and on the knoll, a hill about five hundred to a thousand yards north of the Farm. Simultaneous attacks are now made on these points and all objects gained. About 50 Jaegars prisoners are taken.

20 August 1917

Interrogating prisoners at Divisional Headquarters. The following days are spent chiefly in the back areas but towards the end of the month we again take over and the General decides to move into the advance Brigade HQ in **Lempire** as we anticipate that a concentration on the knoll may come at any time and it is better to be on the scene of action.

One of these days **Merindan**, **General Frank's** ADC, rings up that he is going into **Amiens** for provisions. I obtain permission and go with him. We have a glorious time in **Amiens** and visit the cathedral.

We pick up **Sir R. Alexander** and the Divisional APM (minus his armband) and wend our way to the Golbert Restaurant and have a splendid but expensive luncheon, beautifully served. We shop in the market then proceed to 'Charlies' Bar', the noted cocktail place and consume a few excellent and weird cocktails.

We miss our way on the return journey, not on account of the cocktails as the chauffeur is driving, and find that we have landed near **Soyecourt** and have to strike north over bad roads, through **Roisel** and up to **Ronssoy** and **Lempire**.

31 August 1917

Dawn. I am aroused from my wire bed by a fearful bombardment and as we have been on tenterhooks for several days about the German attack on our positions at the knoll, we feel instinctively that it has come. I go up with **Ross** to find out what is happening. We arrive at Battalion HQ in F. post. It is a very small dugout and is full of people, the Colonel, the adjutant (**Tadman**), **Capt. Priquant** who has just had a marvellous escape on account of a piece of trench mortar sticking in his cigarette case. **Bell** has just come down very much shaken. **Lachlan** has been killed fighting wonderfully. **Rose** and several others are either killed or missing. The knoll is an isolated post five hundred yards in front of the old front line and was held by two companies. Under cover of a heavy bombardment the enemy attacked on all sides overwhelming the garrison who were being relieved at the time. **Battishill's** company (Y) makes a counter-attack in which **Sowry** is killed, the attack is unsuccessful. After returning to report I make my way to the OP from which I can see the Germans in the captured trenches on the knoll.

1 September 1917
The Brigade is relieved and we return to our old camp at **Agicourt**, where we have five days rest.

6 September 1917
We take over the **Epehy** sector. This is just north of the knoll and stretches from **Honnecourt Wood,** shown below [in original], one of the longest sectors we have held yet. Our Brigade Headquarters is in a number of shanties built behind a high railway embankment.

7 September 1917
I proceed to the centre sector. I am busy in the office with air photographs in the afternoon.

8 September 1917
I am on the way with **Rycroft** to see **Murray**, on cycles. On the railway crossing we are stopped by three Americans, Railway Engineer Officers, who are having a rest from their duties, being Sunday, and they have come up the Line to see things. As we are busy we give them a pass to **Col. Heathcote** of the Royal Scots. We have a good walk round the Line. Everything is quiet. We pass through **Villers-Guislain**. This used to be a very hot place but appears to have quietened down nowadays. **Rycroft** has a couple of shots with his walking stick gun at some partridges but misses.

On our arrival back, we find that the Americans are in the mess: they thank us properly. They have been round with **Col. Heathcote** and have been taken into No-Man's-Land by the Sunken Road. This is not under observation from the Boche and is perfectly safe - unless he shells. Two of the HLs spotted them and fired thinking they were Germans, they missed however. The Americans are very elated as they think they were German bullets. They're good fellows and want us to visit their mess in **Péronne.**

9 September 1917
I visit the DLI [Durham Light Infantry] in the west.

10 September 1917
I take **Thompson**, GSO3, round the Royal Scots Trenches.

13 September 1917
The Germans attempted to raid the West Yorks in the Birdcage but were successfully repulsed. The trench mortar barrage was heavy and **Jenkinson** was hit on the steel helmet by a "blind" trench mortar shell. Marvellous escape, only his nose was cracked.

14 September 1917
Nothing particular doing today. **Rycroft** is going up tonight to examine wire in front of the Birdcage.

16 September 1917
We are relieved by the 105th Brigade and return to **Agicourt.**

22 September 1917
The Corps Commander, **General Moreland,** presented ribbands to medal winners. **Battishill** gets his bar to the MC.

23 September 1917
Captain Thompson goes on leave and so calls round with **Merindan** in the car. We go to **Amiens** and have a good time. Golbert for lunch. We visit the market in the afternoon but find very little. The main shops are closed.

26 September 1917
I go on leave. I ride my pony as far as **Péronne** and wait at the railway bridge until I am picked up by a Maxwell car. We go at some speed along the good main road. I am told that we must not stop, if we do we shall not be able to start her again.
    I spend the night at the **Hotel du Rheine, Amiens.**

27 September 1917
I have caught the 11.22 from **Amiens** and am speeding away to **Boulogne**. We travel for some distance along the pretty **River Somme,** there are roses still in the gardens which skirt the river and here and there the river widens and is filled with waving rushes. The country as soon as **Abbéville** is passed becomes bleak and towards **Boulogne** there are the famous sand dunes on which the Bull Ring, the Machine Gun School, and other noted training places are situated. I am in time for the boat but my ticket is dated for the following day so I ask the AMLO, the notorious Major of the Blue

hat if I may go today. I am informed that I may if there is room. Ecstasy – I am aboard. Now for ten days of bliss.

LEAVE IN LEEDS, 28 September to 8 October 1917

RETURN TO FRANCE, Arras and Ypres areas, 8 October 1917 to
19 January 1918

8 October 1917
I return from leave and spend the night at the Hotel de Louvre, **Boulogne.**

9 October 1917
My train has arrived at **Mont St Eloi** and I learn that the brigade is at **Agnez lès Duisans,** the adjoining village to **Duisans** in which we billeted when we were previously at **Arras.**

The division will move shortly to **Ypres**. I cannot say that I am over-joyed at the news. **Rycroft** tells me that the General's application for my retention at the Brigade has not gone through as my post at the Brigade is merely an attachment and not an appointment, so sick at heart I am shortly to rejoin my Battalion which has received instructions to leave the division and become air-analyst with another battalion.

10 October 1917
I apply formally for the Intelligence Corps as Branch Intelligence Officer attached to the Flying Corps for Interpretation of air photos. Whether I shall be accepted remains to be seen.

11 to 13 October 1917
We are merely awaiting instructions for the move. I ride over with **Euselene** and **Allan** to the Ordnance stores at **Dainville.**

14 October 1917
We entrain and arrive at **Arneke** near **Cassel** [as Cassell] proceeding on foot to **Rubrouck** [as **Rudbroreck**].

During the evening I visit the battalion and have dinner and New Market with them.

15 October 1917
Hearing that we do not entrain tomorrow I take the opportunity of cycling over to **Cassel** to see **Cyril Bingham.**

Cassel is a large village situated on an isolated hill commanding wide

views of the surrounding country from the vicinity of the distant front line
to **St Omer** and round to the sea at **Dunkerque** which can be discerned on
a clear day. **Cassel** with its old cobbled streets is crowned (?) with a cream
painted casino at present occupied by 2nd Army Headquarters. I enquire
here for **Cyril** and find that he is at the **St Sylvestre Capell**, a village in the
plain about three miles away to the east. I take a trap leaving my bike at
Cyril's office on the railway. After a short chat he brings me back in his
box van and I pedal back to **Rubrouck/Rudbroreck.**

16 October 1917

We exercise at **Arneke** and proceed in a circular route through **Bergues,** a
fine old fortress near **Dunkerque** to **Proven**. **Proven** is an uninteresting
place, camps being the only shelter; there are no billets.

17 October 1917

We march to **De Wippe Cabaret** [De Wippe's Tavern] and are now in
Belgium. The village comprises only an inn and a few houses but it is pos-
itively swarming with hutments and encampments. We take over from the
guards and have a small camp in **Henley Wood.**

18 October1917

Marching via **Elverdinghe,** we proceed to the Line. What a dismal country this part of Belgium is; the road from **Elverdinghe** to **Boesinghe** is nearly straight and at either side the flat fields are strewn with ammunition
dumps, and wagon lines. Gaunt skeletons of trees shelter twelve-inch guns
whose wicked muzzles point towards the heavens and periodically belch
forth flames. In front of us is the **Pilken Ridge** recently in the hands of the
Boche but from which he must have had a wonderful view of our part of the
plain. The road itself is a mass of traffic; staff cars, motor lorries, ambulances, ammunition carts and mules, platoons of troops marching up and
down, black men on either side shifting shells or unloading, Chinese men
erecting huts, Labour Corps crocks scraping mud off the road, a stray mule
here and there and at the side a little **Decanville** railway ploughing its way
up the line with its supply of ammunition and R.E. materials.

We pass through **Boesinghe** and are just about to pass over the canal,
when overhead appear about ten German Gothas with their scouts making
straight in our direction. All the guns which have been very busy cease firing so as not to be given away by their flashes. The anti-aircraft guns start.
The traffic stops and piles into the side of the road. "Wumph! Wumph!"
two bombs. "Throw yourselves down men," and we all drop down and bury
our faces in the mud just in time, "Wumph! Wumph! Wumph!" and six

bombs drop just on our right and pieces buzz unpleasantly near. As if to change this pleasant game, he drops half a dozen more on the left of the road with a 'dud' in the centre about ten yards away. Having hoped that he has settled most of the traffic on the road, he passes over and drops the remainder of his store in the surrounding quagmire where many of our troops are drawn up preparatory to relieving the front line. Very few casualties were reported and in our area only one man was hit.

We proceed up the **Langemarck [Langhemarcq]** road as far as it goes before turning to the right; we then take a left turn along a plank road. On either side of this the mud is terrible; scarcely an inch of flat ground remains, all is undulating shell holes; here and there a mule or horse lies with its back legs straight up in the air and its front legs crossed having slipped off the planking in places and is difficult to save on account of the mud. In front is the **Forest of Houethulst [Houthulst]** still in possession of the Boche who apparently has every inch of the road taped down by his artillery.

We take over at **Fourck Farm,** a series of three or four concrete pill boxes which are used as a brigade headquarters. They are German pill boxes and the doorways unfortunately point towards the enemy but this has been obviated to a certain extent by the building of a concrete wall a few yards in front of the door.

A row of 60-pounders is just outside the dugout, worse luck.

19 October 1917, [written as 'Oct. 18']

We knew that those blasted guns would do the trick as their huge white flash can be distinguished for miles. The Hun has started; for an hour we have been receiving an eight inch shell every three minutes. We keep well within the walls. One gun is out of action, house across the road, shortly another is in a position similarly. The General telephones to Division regularly requesting them to order the battery away, 'why they should plant themselves down on our doorstep of his headquarters he doesn't know.'

The guns are being moved but are all knocked out in the process; meanwhile we are trying to think of anything but shells and find it difficult as old eight inchers still carry on at three minutes per shell. This is monotonous, 25 yards away, rather near that, 50 yards, better that time, 100 yards gad he's shortening – whooo plonk and a bally eight inch lands on the dugout top and the whole concrete top sways like a boat, for after all it is only built on mud.

We look at one another and laugh – it isn't a brave 'laugh at the danger laugh' it's the usual kind that everyone laughs when a shell bursts near him. There is a nice chunk of stuff chipped off the top. Behind us and attached to our concrete pillbox is an elephant shelter, a corrugated iron arched roof covered with sandbags to a depth of several feet. The next shell misses us and dives straight into this and bursts in the middle of about thirty men. We thought it had gone over but a wild shriek goes up and men come running in from all directions. What a shambles!! With the exception of one man everyone is either killed or wounded. Twenty-nine of them. Some we know they will never find. We bring in the wounded to our pill box and attend to them as well as we can until stretchers arrive. One poor fellow is shot clean through the stomach, he won't live more than a few hours; another is hit through the lungs "let me get away from here" he shrieks "let me get away from here" until the dugout re-echoes it. Still the monotonous shells drop every three minutes either 25, 50 or 100 yards away. Even if we had thought of clearing we couldn't do so until these fellows are out of the way.

We are to be relieved tonight owing to the condition of things generally as Brigade go in for two days only, two days back and so on.

The relieving general says he won't take over from us at **Fourch Farm** but is making his HQ at **Wood 15** and would be pleased if we would hand over to him there. We remove and I am thankful. The General congratulates me, though goodness knows I have been scared out of my wits.

After waiting a few hours in **Wood 15, General Merindan** turns up and we try to find our way to [its] canal bridge; this is most difficult owing to the darkness of the night. Boche is shelling the bridge so we try to find another route and succeed eventually in making **Boesinghe Cross** roads where a car is waiting for us.

I might have mentioned that during the day an officer from the French Division working on our left called in to see us at **Fourch Farm**. After dilating at length on the merits of the French First Division saying that we need have no fear for our flank, he complimented our Brigade upon its success in the front line. In taking his departure he saluted us all in turn 'adieu, mon General' and so on down to the orderly sergeant who was frightfully bucked.

20 October 1917
At **Zoomer Bloom** Cabaret, a fortified house in the **De Wippe - Elverdinghe** road.

26 October 1917
The Brigade goes into the line again but I remain at details to help **Allan.**

27 October 1917
The Brigade entrains at **Boesinghe** for **Proven.** I billet for the Brigade and fix our HQ at **Poona Camp**.

28 October 1917
I watch a German bomber nearly brought down at midday. In this district the enemy is over every night dropping tons of bombs.

29 October 1917
I visit the 17th [West Yorks] who are playing the Scottish Borderers at football.

30 October 1917
March to **De Wippe Cabaret (Beuson's Farm)** [De Wippe's Tavern], quite a nice asbestos hut similar to Kendles at Fyling Hall [Yorkshire]. **Rycroft** has **Col. Fortune** of the Black Watch in to dinner. Old Boche drops bombs.

1 November 1917
Wood 15. They find they didn't get on very well without the Intelligence Officer as the Division were always ringing up for reports and **Rycroft** having other work to do couldn't be bothered with them.

2 November 1917
Up the line.

4 November 1917
We march back to **Proven** and remain there for a few hours. I go to **Poperinghe** for supplies. I am detailed for two days at an aeroplane photograph class at No 9 aerodrome. I call in at 5th Army HQ re photographs job. The army HQ are admirably chosen. The mansion is of white stone and square built and rather ugly but is situated in the centre of a park surrounded by a very wide belt of copper beeches such as I have never seen in my life before. It is like a scene from a theatre. Here and there under the trees are dotted the various staff officers' huts for such people as cannot be accommodated in the chateau.

8 November 1917
We take over **Pitt Camp** on the north side of **Proven.** We are amused at the names given to the various casualty stations in the district and at first glance they appear to be Belgian names i.e. Bandaghem, Dosinghem, Curinghem, etc.

We receive instructions that the 17th West Yorks are not to proceed with the Brigade but that until further notice they are to hold themselves in readiness to be amalgamated with the 15th. West Yorks (Leeds Pals).

I leave the Brigade and join the Battalion Mess which is rather a drafty [draughty] hut in **Porchester Camp. Major Gill** DSO is in command - so we kick our heels until we are told to proceed to **Elverdinghe.** We are billeted in the house just south of the railway at **Zoomer Bloom.**

25 November 1917
We hold a church parade in the Salvage Tent.

26 November 1917
Railways proceeding splendidly. The 17th Division is in the line and the 35th Division just south. I have just been over to **Brielen** to see the Brigade.

30 November 1917
We are awakened in the very early morning by Perishing Pavey who has been pretty near us several times, and this time, I am afraid, a shell has dropped clean into a tent occupied by the signallers killing poor **Corporal West** and **Sergeant Hemsley.**

1 December 1917
We move today. I go ahead with my billeting party on cycles to **Godewaersveldt** - I can't spell it - and am told by the town mayor of that place that we are to billet at **Thieushouck.** This is a pretty little village.

Our mess has a piano and we are happy.

2 December 1917
We march to **Merville. Umbers** and I have horses and we successfully billet the troops. I call in later to see an old peasant with whom you will find **Cohen** and I stayed during our second spell at **Le Sart** in 1916. He remembers me and greatly mourns the loss of poor old **Cohen.**

I dine with the Boys at the Hotel de Ville Restaurant at night.

3 December 1917
Umbers and I ride to **L'Eclamée** (near **Chocgues**).

4 December 1917
We proceed to **Barlin,** and put practically the whole battalion into three billets. About quarter of an hour before the troops march in, the town, which

is about nine miles from the line, is shelled and as this happens every few months all the women and children evacuate it. The roads are full of people streaming out until the shelling is over. One or two shells drop quite close to our men's billets and I am wondering whether it is safe just yet.

The Battalion has arrived - the shelling is less frequent and the civilians are returning. The miners, for it is a mining district, nearly all are much the worse for drink; the shelling apparently makes them want a reviver and they are being escorted home by their wives. It would be rather humorous if it wasn't so pathetic.

5 December 1917
We reach **Acq,** our destination; the 15th Battalion West Yorkshire (Leeds Pals) is about two miles away at **Mont St Eloi** and we are to amalgamate.

6 December 1917
A number of men who have given their names for the tank corps leave us, as well as some of the officers. They at any rate will probably have about six months in Blighty.

7 December 1917
The Battalion less **Major Gill, Lawton, Evans, Westcott, Fry,** myself and one or two others, marches off to join the 15th. **Major Gill** has decided that those who were specialists will stand a better chance of securing similar work if they go with him to the base and are then sent up to other Battalions as specialists.

9 December 1917
Lawton goes on leave.

10 December 1917
Major Gill is to report at the Base. **Westcott** and **Fry** are to be attached for accommodation and rations to the 18th West Yorks, **White** and myself are attached to the 16th West Yorks and are billeted with C Company. **Garburt** is posted to this battalion and so are **Evans** and **Battishill.** We have rather an unpleasant interview with the **Colonel** who thinks that we have been posted and not attached. Trust they won't post us.

21 December 1917
After having had a good time here, I am posted with **Thurgood, White** and **Westcott** to the 12th Battalion which I understand is a storm Battalion.

We recollect that our old Lewis Gun Sergeant, **Robinson,** is the adjutant

First World War British tank. By permission of the IWM, neg. no. Q5572. The first battle to use many tanks was at Cambrai.

so we shall have a friend at court. We are greeted by **Robinson** and posted to our companies. I go to D Company.

22 December 1917

We move to **Mory**. Our job during the next few days is to do six solid hours wiring in front of the line at **Bullencourt.** During the evening we march up in platoons at a hundred yards interval, draw spades and wiring apparatus at **Ecuist** and make for **Station Redoubt.** The 12th have a new system of wiring which is very speedy when one is used to it. The G.HQ staff have evidently got the wind up with regard to the projected Boche offensive. This work is being carried out as far as I can understand from the [North] Sea to Switzerland. All passes off well after a very quiet night. The initial stages are done.

23 December 1917

Similar work, another belt of wire is being put out. 1,400 yards of wire have been erected tonight exceeding that of our expert pioneers by 600 yards.

24 December 1917

At it again.

25 December 1917 Christmas Day.

We are not going to do any more tonight, so we all make as merry as we can. The snow has been falling heavily and we are in a large draughty wooden hut with an apology for a door at either end and the draught is scurrying through exploring all the corners and scarcely adding to the enjoyment of the occupants who are gathered round the iron stove. **MCate** is preparing a 'rum punch' for consumption after the dinner. Most of us have received parcels and have thus contributed towards the mess funds and we are really having quite a good time. **MCate** is a little — ! and I am afraid the rum punch suffers in consequence, still it isn't bad and warms us up ready for our valises.

26 December 1917

We finish our wiring and are congratulated by the General. This evening hasn't been quite a pleasure and the old Hun is gently playing upon us with 4.2s, not causing any casualties upon the company but making us duck pretty often. He has caught one party on the dump and knocked them about rather badly. We can hear one fellow shrieking his hardest. We make up our minds to go quickly past the dump when we have finished our work.

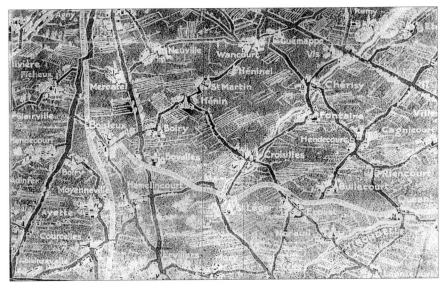

A French map from 5 January 1918, south of Arras.

Arras - The museum with all its riches is destroyed.

1 January 1918

Our job being done we travel to **Boisleux** and camp next to the 13th Kings where I meet 'Froggy' or Louis as he is now known, **Mons. Dehaene** my old French Master at Wellington College.

We are to train for a month which is delightful. I am to take over Battalion Intelligence Work. We spend quite a good three weeks here and have several visits to 34th Div. Pantomime now running in a large French hut at **Boisleux.** Call at **Arras** several times.

We are now to start digging the Corps south of **Wancourt** and half the battalion goes up every night. In due course we relieve the people in the Front Line and take over the Reserve Line between **Héninel** and **Wancourt.**

This is the original **Hindenburg Line** and has a series of most remarkable dugouts. Down in the ground about 60 feet runs a gallery honeycombed at intervals with dugouts. This gallery passes for miles and I understand throughout the whole system. In some places it is wide and in others only just passable. It eventually crosses over No-Man's-Land and is occupied by the Germans at the other side being of course blocked up between. Throughout the entire work an elaborate electric light system is adopted run by petrol motors at intervals. Gas shells are suspended at the foot of each flight of stairs with a cord to the sentry above as a warning of gas.

Here and there outside the line are concrete pillboxes, some shattered, others apparently untouched. In the distance is one of our stranded tanks. Poor **Philip Hersch** VC was killed a few yards away from our dugout entrance.

Arras - General view of the Town Hall after the bombardment.

In the course of a few days we take over the frontline from the 4th Fusiliers. The line runs just east of **Chérisey** which is in German hands, then down to **La Fontaine-lès-Croisilles.** In the distance further north we see the heights of **Monchy-le-Preux**, taken by cavalry after heavy losses, and ever since a longed for hope of the Germans as such valuable observation can be gained of our lines from the summit. Further over is one of the German ridges and the **Arras – Cambrai** road passing near **Vis-en-Artois.**

All our energies are upon the defence and we can see swarms of Germans from one of our O.Ps. Periodic bombardments take place and trench mortar strafes.

G.H.Q. has warned us that an attack by gas projectiles is likely to come off in a few days as from prisoner information and from observation we know that projectors are being installed.

We are unceremoniously called from our sleep by a heavy bombardment; we are now in support, all kinds of lights are going up, the bombardment travels north and south yet no attack seems to come. We arrive at the conclusion that both sides have the wind up.

The Batallion is going to be broken up under the three battalions in a Brigade System.

A few passes for six month tours in **England** are expected to come through in a few days.

We re-visit **Arras,** and look up our old haunts. **Westcott** and I leave for England, stay en route with **Madame Varley Herberts,** 93 Rue des Veillards, **Boulogne.**

INTELLIGENCE TRAINING IN ENGLAND, Jan. – Oct. 1918

After a month's leave we both join the 15th Essex at Yarmouth. I am sent on a Company Commanders' course at Brocton where I fortunately come out top and when I get back am handed over a Company of 1,045 men and my acting captaincy. After a strenuous time, not without interest, I report to Folkestone on October 16, 1918.

RETURN TO FRANCE, nearing the Armistice, 16 Oct. – Nov. 1918
16 October 1918

Westcott and I are instructed by the AMLO at **Boulogne** to report to the 8th West Yorks (Leeds Rifles) and as our train will not go until the day after tomorrow **Westcott, Gaudy** (who is going to the Hampshires) and I fix up rooms at **Mme Herberts,** where we have a royal time and only report once to **St Martius Camp** to have our gas masks fitted. We look round the Cathedral, Castle and the Walls from which the first Channel balloon flight was made.

After entraining for several days we arrive at **Cambrai** and get a motor lorry as far as **Carnières** where the VI Corps Officers' Club is situated. The Barber attends to our various wants as we are pretty frosty.

During the day another lorry lands us near to **Bévillers.** The Battalion is doing a stint at **Solesmes** and comes out successfully having captured the village, prisoners and guns.

[Gap in diary]

25 October 1918

We attend a Brigade Presentation of medal ribbons. **Harrison** receives his M.C. [Military Cross]. It is an order in the Brigade that we do not carry sticks. The Devons have arrived with sticks and about five minutes before the General is due to arrive the Sergeant Major walks past the officers collecting their sticks to the concealed amusement of the troops.

26 October 1918

We pay another visit to the Pelicans who I may say are the Divisional Pierrot Troop and a splendid performance they give too. **Jimmy Rich** of the Empire Farm is the black comedian.

28 October 1918

We have a company scheme of attack across cabbage fields. The cabbages are extremely fine and the largest I have ever seen.

30 October 1918

We hear that **Turkey** has signed the **Armistice** and do not think that **Germany** will go on much longer.

31 October 1918

Pelicans again – we might as well have as much amusement as possible.

1 November 1918

White has just gone on a Lewis Gun Course. I take over the Company pro tem.

2 November 1918

Bathing in the morning.

3 November 1918

We prepare to move up and march in the dark to **Solesmes,** where we arrive at 7.30pm. It is a much bigger place than I thought. Persistent Percy starts at night.

4 November 1918

The Colonel goes on leave. We join messes with D Company but march to **Escarmain** at night and after a few hours sleep we leave again.

Received a pencil message on squared paper:

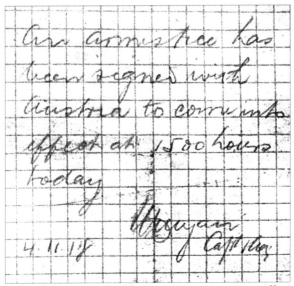

An armistice has been signed with Austria to come into effect at 1500 hours today. (signed) ? Captain, 4.11.18

5 November 1918

4.30am. The weather is glorious. The large attack is to take place at 5.30 and we are present in Divisional Reserve. The guns have just commenced this barrage and the horizon in German lines has become a wonderful display of fireworks, red, green, yellow, white, golden and so on. In a few minutes the Hun is retaliating; a few heavy shells drop in our vicinity, one on the road just behind our company fortunately doing little damage. A 5.9 has dropped into a dump of Very lights which are throwing out their traces of fire in every direction.

We arrive in the avenue west of **Ruesnes** - all around us are heavy guns belching fire. After an hour or so strings of prisoners come down and Divisional Red Tabs with tin hats charge up in front of us so that we are now sure the Boche [is] rapidly retreating. Supply tanks arrive with their cargoes of ammunition and gradually the guns around us die down as the Huns are out of range. We feverishly await an order to move. On our right we hear the firing of machine guns in the direction of **Le Guesnoy.**

At last the call has come and we move through **Ruesnes** up over the original front line where the bodies of several machine gunners lie huddled together. On our right we can just see the chimneys of **Le Guesnoy**. The town is surrounded by New Zealanders but it has not yet surrendered; at this moment a rapid fire of machine guns is kept up, intermingled now and then with the discharge of a field gun battery which appears to have been left behind.

We halt in a little orchard in a ravine and have a meal; a small cottage near by contains the bodies of several Germans who have remained behind to snipe.

We move on to **Orsinval** and up the village street and here and there gaunt Germans have paid the price and lie outstretched upon the pavements.

Our C.O. comes back to meet us, as we are strung out at intervals, and informs us that we are to attack immediately. The front line is about three miles ahead and we are to go through and attack up to a certain point. I am now busy making my plans and placing my platoons in their allotted positions. As usual in warfare, another order has arrived that we are to attack in the morning instead of now and we form up in a small defile and dig ourselves in the bank for the night. It doesn't take Tommy long to put up a comfortable bit of shelter and all the entrenching tools are being rapidly employed in scooping out a hollow in the bank to get the body into. An old German gun pit provides a certain amount of corrugated iron and with this on top of us we don't fare so badly!

Company Commanders are sent off to reconnoitre the roads for our attack and we arrive at forward battalion H.Q. a few hours after dusk has fallen. The road is rough with shell holes and many horses, carts and rifles, so apparently many men have been hit by the fire of our guns in the morning. Everything seems fairly quiet now but the uneven, scary nature of the road makes us feel that we are walking on a danger spot, and the hair of our heads is ready to stand on end at any moment. Mine nearly always does. After chatting with the C.O. of K.O.Y.L.I.s we return, running the gauntlet of a few shells but not coming to any harm.

Our camp is asleep and after about a quarter of an hour's searching I find **Oates** in his 'bivy' and join him. We have about four hour's sleep and are up at 4.30 [6 Nov.]

Pencil message on squared paper reads:
O.C. ALL COYS.
The 185 Inf. Bdi. are continuing the advance tomorrow on the Divl. Front to the high ground on the line approx N8 central – LE CHEVAL BLANC – LE GRAND SART.

The 1/5 Devon Regt. will be on the right, the 12/20 London Regt on the left.

The 8th W.Y.R. will be in support and will move to assembly positions in the vicinity of the cross roads at M15CO5. O C Coys will report with their Coys at N 15C 05 at the following times:

      B. Co. 5.30 hours tomorrow
      C. Co. 5.35   "   "
      D. Co. 5.40   "   "
      A. Co. 5.45   "   "
      H.Q.Co. 5.45   "   "

The four Lt. Ambers tool wagon and H.Q. limber will report at M15CO5 at 5.36 hours. Pack animals and riding horses will remain in their present location.

Route to assembly position LA BELLE MAISON road running through M14a b and d to M15CO5.

Zero hour guns 5.11.18
Acknowledge
     22.50   4.11.18   (signed) ?, Capt.

6 November 1918
And after a stiff dose of rum, which gladdens our hearts, and a nip of tea and biscuits, we move on to cross roads of **Petit Marais** where we wait until the dark has gone and longer. At 7.30am we are still waiting, and news

comes down that the Boche has gone goodness knows where. We still wait. Motor lorries now keep coming up; a sure sign that something has happened. At last we move on a mile or so and stand on a ridge overlooking the village of **Gommegnies** about three miles away. The plain is well wooded and away on our right lies the **Forest of Mormal**. Large columns of smoke are rising from various places behind the trees and there we can locate the homesteads of the poor French inhabitants.

After some difficulty in getting across the railway for the bridge has been mined, we push on in artillery formation, through several villages in which large German guns lie fast in the mud or damaged by our shells; a few civilians, very shaken wave us onward singing the *Marseillaise* and giving us apples; my pockets are full. You will hear the British Tommy saying how mean the French and Belgians are yet they don't realise that some of our men are ahead of them and have already received gifts; these gifts cannot last for ever, the poor French peasant has had all her cows etc. taken and the only thing left is a little coffee, a little bread and a few apples, and the Lord knows she gives these away generously enough as long as they last.

Many improvised bridges have to be made for our limbers over streams where the road bridges have been blown in to impede our advance. We reach a little village called the **Cheval Blanc,** billet the men in a barn and then partake of food which the French people give us. Just a bit of bread, brown and unsavoury, a little coffee and a few pears. We give them in exchange a little white bread, at the sight of which one old woman nearly has hysterics, and a little corned beef. We can't spare much as we don't know when we shall get our next rations.

We are instructed to form up on the north eastern edge of **Mormal Forest** and pass through A and D Companies, who are at present occupying the front posts. Our positions are gained at about 4.20 and the KOYLIs on our left and also the Guards have been repulsed and machine gun fire is extremely heavy. I am of the opinion that if we attack practically the whole of two companies will be wiped out. I go over to the village with my runner in search of **Nesbit,** O.C. B Coy., and we both agree that the attack would be a failure. I immediately despatch runners to the CO explaining the position and stating that a much better advantage will be gained in the early morning with our artillery barrage and that we are until instructed further placing ourselves under the command of A and D Companies.

In the course of the night this action is approved of and we are to carry the stunt out at 6.0 in the morning when the barrage will commence. The night is beastly, we have a certain amount of fun in trying to find our pickets in the dark and do not succeed in locating **Oates** until an hour before we

move off. Machine gun fire through the night has been heavy and the bullets have fortunately been mostly above our heads, though several men have
been hit. It is an eery feeling in the dark when 'whu-ee' and a bit of a
branch falls at your feet.

7 November 1918

6am. The guns are setting up a barrage which aids us wonderfully in keep-
ing direction in this very close country. We have found several of the
machine gun positions and their placing bears out my theory of being wiped
out and also the fact that the Germans are fast retreating.

My company is in support and on the capture of **Obies** we are to pass
through A Company and form the front attack. This is successfully managed and we pass through the above mentioned company and take the village of **Tayompret.** Old **Oates** captures a few Germans and we have little
resistance. The principal firing is on our left where the Londons are having
a roughish time. The buildings are searched and I make my Company Head
Quarters at a farm in the village. The civilians, rather scared to death, come
up from the cellars and hand us coffee which the French always have stew-
ing upon the hob or the long stoves which are generally used. They seem
delighted to see us and give us anything within their means. They talk
together about the youth of the officers and many a time I hear, "Ah, le
Capitain, si jeune, si jeune" and I feel rather bucked.

We have posted sentry groups or piquets in front of us then settle down
for the night until we get further news. The Boche guns have evidently
found a temporary resting place and have once more started shelling us. I
get a few winks of sleep and am trying a few more when an urgent message
for me to attend a conference at HQ arrives. In the meantime another battalion passes through us.

 Squared paper with pencil note:
"Adjutant
Artillery have taken up position in front and rear of our lines and our rifle
posts are full of water.

May we withdraw men from trench and leave a post to give warning of
any unusual occurrences where companies will immediately occupy original posts."
(signed) **E. Raymond Hepper Lt.**

8 November 1918

After trying a short cut - about three times as long - I arrive at Battalion HQ
in **Obies** at about 2.30am where I learn that we are to form up at the cross-

roads at 4.30am. We rush back and gather our men together and meet at the cross-roads. Our march then commences and we pass through **Mecquignies** and again form up at **Cheneau Loup [=Quène-au-Leu]** and attack the **Bois Delahaye** at 6am. The barrage is effective and the Germans with the exception of a few dead ones have disappeared. The wood is very dense and **Oates** taking his company steers his way through the centre. I and my headquarters choose the right hand edge of the wood as it should be the easiest place to find us in case orders are given and one should always know where to be found.

We arrive on the objective, the main road through the wood, and I post my band. We are a heterogeneous collection - **C. Sergt. Major Stead** arrived with a revolver, four stretcher bearers unarmed, four runners with rifles, my servant with a rifle and myself with a revolver so that in case we are attacked we are not too formidable; heavy machine gun fire is now going on at the left hand side of the wood and a certain amount of shouting. Leaving **Sergt Major Stead** in charge of the right, I charge off with **Robertshaw** my servant to find what it is all about. I arrive just as **Oates** has captured a machine gun and he is after the other one as they generally work in pairs. He has no one on his left so we seem to be in a nice pickle. The remainder of the people appear to be lost in the wood; **Oates** is here with about seventeen men and my HQ with about five rifles are 500 yards away. After about ten minutes the remainder of the company arrives and also a company of Devons who have lost their way in the wood. Piquets are posted and I fix my Headquarters in the Keeper's Cottage and am forced to throw out a flank defence as the Guards on the left have not yet made their appearance; it is now about 10am. The Guards arrive at 5pm.

A and D Companies are expected to leap frog through us but owing to the Hun being reinforced to impede the advance very little is done, and it is not until the Guards come up that any progress can be made. Cold steel is their aid and a German machine gunner lies pierced through the heart. The German artillery has been playing heavily upon the road and a 5.9 has fallen just outside the wall of the house damaging it but fortunately not hurting anyone.

Hand-written message on squared paper:
"Adjutant
Statement of O.C. A Coy. Forwarded by a runner.

D Company are at present at my HQ OC A is here pro tem. where he fixes on his forward HQ runners will be led to him.

I have seen MQ Section who are located at O 12 & 6.7 and have told them to support A Company with covering fire.

Note re SOS acknowledged.

The majority of their questions were answered and despatched at 7.30pm. I presume this has failed to reach you. I am in touch with Guards at 6 and 7. 1.

(signed) E Raymond Hepper. O.C. C Coy."

9 November 1918

We are relieved at 11am and march to **Mecquignies** very tired. During the last four days the division has driven the Hun back nearly twenty miles.

We hear rumours of an armistice and that the white flag has been passed through the lines. The front line is now beyond **Maubeuge.**

10 November 1918

Up at 5.30 and march to **Sous le Bois** one of the suburbs of **Maubeuge.** On the way during one of the halts we talk to an old man and his wife who bring their chairs for the officers to sit on. The C.O. calls all the company commanders to pass down the news that the **Kaiser** has abdicated and that no sign of the Boche can be found just in front of us. The old man calls out "Vive les Anglais" and the old woman bursts into tears of joy.

We march on to strains of Tipperary. Strange that we should be covering the old ground of the **Battle of Mons** again just as an armistice is being declared.

In the doorway of a little cottage stands a bearded aged man at the salute; on his breast are medals and in his cap are feathers just such as children put in their paper hats when playing at soldiers. The old fellow is singing at the top of his voice and our men begin to laugh when it suddenly strikes them that he is singing the *Marseillaise*, the band carries on the strain and it is picked up by the men and so we are making our entry.

We have a good billet. In fact the woman takes the things off her bed saying that she is going to a neighbour's so that we can have her rooms. It is no good arguing.

11 November 1918

Hostilities ceased at 11 o'clock. The woman at the billet is highly pleased when I tell her and she catches me under the chin with both hands and kisses me, much to the amusement of our servants who dance and scream with laughter.

12 November 1918

We have received the terms of the armistice which I read out to the parade. There is very little exuberance.

13 November 1918

We have a brigade parade and a speech by our **Brigadier General Lord Hampden.**

15 November 1918

I have a look round **Maubeuge.** It is a fortified town surrounded by moats and walls; the church has been decorated with flowers and a screen of red, white and blue behind the altar. There is nothing of exceptional interest beyond the high prices.

A ring of forts about four miles apart surround the town and these were blown up by the French before the retreat in 1914.

White has returned and takes over the company. I am pleased that I have had permission to command the Company during the last offensive.

MARCH across South Eastern BELGIUM into GERMANY for OCCUPATION near COLOGNE, November 1918 - January 1919

16 November 1918

We start our great march to Germany proceeding south of **Maubeuge** to **Ferrière-le-Grand.**

The roads are full of returning British, French and Italian prisoners, who have walked many miles. The Germans merely opened the prison encampment gates and said 'clear' or whatever ugly sounds their language means for that word. No food – that is begged from the wayside cottages until our own lines are reached, where military police point the way to large dumps of provisions placed at convenient spots. They are a weary crowd, unshaven and hitherto uncared for. Frenchmen with British caps and haversacks, British with French overcoats, Italians with all three, a fag or two picked up from the passing troops, feet wrapped in puttees or old cloths where boots have been worn out or taken by the Germans; a sorry lot all with our instruction namely to get well through the Allies' Lines.

The censorship is now relaxed. My French comes in handy and I am called in by a pretty girl to attend to her dog whose leg has been broken. I can do nothing for it and leave after trying to console a tearful maiden. When I get back I find I have lost my pipe and I must have left it at the house. I am greatly rotted that I did it on purpose. It is a myth.

17 November 1918

I attend church as it is Sunday.

18 November 1918

March to **Bousignies**, a one-eyed village and billet in a cheerless house from which all the furniture has been removed.

We are now in a district where the British and Prussian forces met the French before Waterloo and we have been within a few miles of the village of **Beaumont** where **Napoleon** had his Headquarters. I inform the men of this, thinking that they would be interested to hear this; one of the fellows replies: "By gum but we've got 'em on the 'op now 'aven't we Sir."

19 November 1918

I am left behind to report on the tidiness of the billets and to hand them over to incoming troops. I catch the battalion up at **Gozée**. We pass through **Thouin** [= **Thuin**] a fair sized town which has been decorated with tri-umphal arches and flags. We are intensely surprised to see sweetmeats of all kinds, and the butchers' shops have a plentiful store – then our opinion about starving Germany and Belgium changed. If we had also known the prices we should have got rather a shock.

20 November 1918

Gerpinnes. Being with the rear party I miss the triumphal entry. As in **Thouin** everything is decorated and the Mayor and corporation such as it is, turned out to meet the Battalion; crowds of little children in white formed a procession into which the Mayor smoking a large cigar and the aforesaid corporation joined as well as the town band who amuse our men with their big drum which is strapped to a man's back whilst the drummer walks behind in comfort. All the male population almost immediately afterwards visited the estaminent [tavern] and became too cheery to stand up.

White and I are billeted at the Mayor's where we all have our Company mess. **Harrison** falls madly in love with a pretty little girl at **Henderson's** billet and I am called in to interpret. If interpreters always have this sort of time, I am joining the interpreters' Corps in the next war. She's seventeen and her sister's 22; they always tell you their ages in France and Belgium and want to know yours. I must have told thousands my age. She, we're here again, wears a Belgian Fringe and has most gorgeous eyes and a beau-tiful accent. Her sister, too, is very chic.

We spend three days here and have quite a good time. The Regimental Sergeant Major organises dances in the Town Hall into which you have to shove your way. All the girls in the town seem to be there and don't our boys have a good time.

24 November 1918

We arrive in **Mettet,** in the square of which a hundred guns are parked in accordance [with] the terms of the Armistice. Our rations are now appallingly bad and are about two days behind hand. The provisions have to be brought from **Solesmes** by motor lorries and there is a matter of about fifty miles over exceedingly bad roads. They cannot be brought by train owing to the rails having been removed by the Germans.

We are charmed by a clock in our billet which plays a tune before it strikes the hour.

25 November 1918

Arrived at **Warnant** near the **Meuse,** and billet at a house on the hill belonging to Mr **Joseph Thirau.** My arrival being a little behind that of the others I find myself ushered into their presence in the dining room. There is a sigh of relief as neither **Harrison** nor **Henderson** can talk French. Our host brings out two bottles of Moulin à Vent which he has had hidden underneath his coals in the coal cellar for nearly five years. **Joseph junior** is learning English and so I give him a lesson and we become great friends. Madame and M'lle are also quite nice and we have a good time. In the evening more wine and cigars arrive and we have music; the daughter is playing national airs and we are asked to sing *God Save the King* – all Belgians are very keen on this. Afterwards we sing *Brabracomie* in French! And I promise **Thirau junior** that I would write to him in French if he would write to me in English so as to improve each other.

Belgian bank note.

The view from the windows is magnificent, there is a wonderful valley with wooded hills on either side; little villages cap the hills and small orchards, their trees in long straight rows, make the country look like the picture labels on champagne bottles. It is called **Little Switzerland.**

26 November 1918

Up betimes. We have a long march before us. I am again left behind to attend to the cleanliness of the billets. I fortunately have a cycle. And after having inspected the billets I ride on towards the **Meuse,** a few miles away.

What a noble river! A suspension bridge is thrown across and at the other side the village of **Yvoir** nestles under the limestone cliffs through which the river flows. At the foot of the cliffs the trees are still retaining their autumn tints and contrast with the dark firs which interspace.

After a long climb I come up with the Division on the move. The 8th West Yorks. are well in advance and I ride past the Signal Company, the R.F.A. whose steaming horses show the steepness of the climb, past battalions of infantry, past the field ambulances who are kept fairly busy with the usual number of stragglers on a long march. This brings me to **Spontin.**

Every other house has been burnt down by the Germans in 1914 and their gaunt skeletons stand out as a memorial of organised destruction; as in all other villages decorations and banners are placed across the roads. Our entry is far more pathetic than any I have yet witnessed. The large streamers across the road spell out "Gloire et Honneur aux Vinqueurs qui a liberate la Belgique" and implore us to remember their martyrs and orphans. Out of several houses black flags are flying and a small band of four or five musicians strike up "God Save the King". Never again shall I say that our National Anthem is uninspiring – it is magestic even when played by a few men remaining from among the stricken inhabitants. I am almost crying now, seated on a stone in the side road and feeling that I wouldn't have missed this for all the world – the thanks of a liberated people.

[dated 26 November in diary]

Soret. This is a benighted spot well on top of a steep hill. The people at our billet are not at all affable and the stove in the mess won't burn, blue faces, blue spirits and drizzle.

27 November 1918

I have just cleaned up the billets and the battalion has gone to **Chapois.** I have discovered why the people were so frigid yesterday. They entirely altered this morning and shook hands with us and said Good-bye. It seems that a German Colonel has been billeted with them and he had French girls,

A splendid chateau (St. Roch) near the town of Ciney in south east Belgium visited during the West Yorkshire's march to occupy Germany after the signing of the armistice on 11 November 1918.

whom they had to look after, with him. They probably expected all officers were alike but they soon changed their opinion with regard to us.

We have apparently now got onto one of the German main lines of retreat and we come across the various remains of encampments; the internal arrangements of cattle lie about in the fields near by where they have been slaughtered for a meal. Steel helmets are strewn around everywhere showing how undisciplined were the troops at the latter end of the retreat; huts and buildings are burnt in many places and on the high road burnt motor transport wagons with iron tyres lie in the ditch and in some places have been run down steep banks to break up and in so doing their wheels have rolled in all directions. It would have made a fine kinomatograph picture.

Here and there aeroplanes have been parked in accordance with armistice terms and the station of **Ciney** through which we pass holds two train loads of aeroplane fuselages.

In the course of an hour we arrive at **Chapois**, where we learn we are to stop for a few days owing to the shortage of food supplies. Between **Solesmes** and here there is no railway and the motor convoys have to come a distance of 75 miles. One officer has come up on one of those convoys. Fifty two lorries formed the convoy and on arrival here only twelve were left. The remainder were either bogged or ditched or had engine trouble, so you can imagine that many times the supplies were very sparse.

28 to 30 November 1918
Routine work of cleaning up and parade. We see the first train this side of the Gap.

1 December 1918
Food is very scarce and the company is not on parade at the appointed time; on enquiries we find that until they receive proper food they will not parade. **White** makes a little speech and the men fall in. The transport officer has unfortunately been passing and has taken the report round that C Company has mutinied and we get the C.O., the Major and all sorts of people down. However, all passes off successfully.

2 December 1918
Walking into **Leignon** with **Harrison** and **Fotheby**. There is not very much to see but we are surprised by the display of brass-work in the shop windows. The Boche tried to lay hands on all this alloy and even removed door handles and latches but the shop people have evidently been wily and buried all their stores and immediately brought them to light when the enemy marched away. The same applies to flags, and in many places triumphal arches and allied flags were being erected or being hung out before the rear guards of the German army passed through. There have been many incidents of where the Boche has tried to tear these down but this takes time and time is short.

I endeavour to purchase a cake of soap and a small piece of about 2 inches square costs me 7 francs or between three and four shillings whereas in England before the war it would have been about 3d [three old pence]. I have been trying for the last few days to get soap to wash the men's clothes. All the Belgian women are anxious to do this if we will supply the soap. The army supplies have not come up and there appears to be no soap in Belgium. Vegetables are also very scarce; caramels in paper are a penny each.

3 December 1918

A Brigade Parade is now on but as Company Second-in-Command I have to attend to the Interior[?] Economy of the Company and this takes a certain amount of time.

The Padre comes in to tea.

4 December 1918

We play Banker in the evening. I win 15 francs but **Henderson** and **Harrison** lose heavily and we resolve not to play any more.

5 December 1918

White leaves to be demobilized and I take over the command of the Company.

6 and 7 December 1918

Nothing much doing. **Garlic** and **Robinson** come in to dinner.

We have made friends with a poacher who keeps us supplied with hares and pheasants. This is quite a good scheme and fairly cheap. They cost us about 4 francs each i.e. 2/6 [2 shillings and 6 pence, now 12½ p]

8 December 1918

We were to have moved today but it has been cancelled during the night.

9 December 1918

Motley arrives and becomes Company 2 in C. We have a route march and receive orders to move tomorrow.

10 December 1918

Up at 5.30 and move off at 5.45 and march to **Maffe**. Beastly day. Our Company is providing the Guard which is highly complimented on its turn out.

11 December 1918

An early start. The country is magnificent. The district is very hilly, being similar to Roseberry Topping and the Cleveland Hills [Yorkshire], and they are practically covered from top to foot with spruce and pines [Spruce *Picea abies*; Scots Pine *Pinus sylvestris*].

We rise higher and higher and then on turning a bend in the road we find we can see down into the valley, a rich emerald green, dotted here and there with little red-roofed homesteads at the foot of mighty hills and far below is a road on which is the Battalion preceding us and which we thought miles ahead and then we realise that we are on one of the famous hairpin bends and that we shall shortly be traversing that road. The men, who do not greatly appreciate beauty, start grumbling when they find they have to go at least a mile in a semi-circle to reach that spot directly below us. The bend negotiated, we drop down into the valley through which gurgles a rocky mountain stream given the name of **River l'Ourthe.**

At **Hamoir** we find good billets and also that this is now [a] railhead.

12 December 1918

We have fourteen kilometres in the pouring rain to **Ernonheid**, which village accommodates B Company and our own. We have not struck [well?] this time as we have to march two miles out of our way to get to it and shall have two extra miles tomorrow to get out of it in order to join the Battalion. We are messing with B Company and I always find that this is not a good arrangement.

13 December 1918

Up at 6.0, parading in torrents and we march to **Bass**e-**Bodeux**; owing to the rain the march is uninteresting. The men are all billeted and we have an excellent Company mess. The house is not a large one but I have a big bedroom painted in panels and richly decorated and – a fine big fire in front of which my clothes are drying. The mess is a front room having a plate glass wall.

14 December 1918

Again on trek through **Les Trois-Ponts** and **Grand Halleux** to **Vielsalm**, quite a nice little town where the people cannot do enough for us. The daughter of the house, married to a Belgian officer, spends the evening talking to us and informs us that the **Kaiser** passed through in his car on his way to Holland after his abdication. **The Crown Prince** also passed through and got out of his car to sell his toy dog which someone bought for five francs and Madame was very annoyed that she hadn't bought it. It seems rather a far fetched story though she said it was quite true.

They keep five sheep in the cellar here.

16 December 1918

The officers are rather excited as we are to pass over the German Frontier today.

Poteau – The German Frontier. At the cross roads is a sentry box painted with black and white stripes and the motto "Gott mit uns".

The officers' call is blown and we all troop up and have our photographs [taken], with the sentry box as a background, and we then march on to the strains of Tipperary. The country is open with occasional black patches of fir trees on the hills, for we are still high, and it is very sparsely populated. The roads are bad and have apparently had much heavy traffic on them. We pass through a village called **Recht** and we note the change. There are no flags here, all is quite quiet and we had expected that the people would view us sullenly but would show a certain amount of curiosity but no – everyone goes about his own work in the usual way taking no notice, as if British soldiers were an everyday event, and only the children, who didn't understand, follow us, attracted by the band as a repetition of the Pied Piper of Hamlin.

All the children wear the German forage cap as I understand that as the Germans passed near their own villages and homes, they fell out and demobilised themselves, showing how their morale stood in the closing days. I mention the children – I have never seen so many in my life, every house appears to have about nine and as we pass along these seem to peep out of every window in the houses; no wonder Germany has had a number of spare men to throw away in mass formation attacks. The majority seem to be boys.

We are now passing through a dense forest of pine trees which makes the road on either side seem bounded by a wall of darkness; here and there at the bye-roads are sign posts edged with black for everything seems to be black and white so far, even the houses and the clouds seem ready to pour down showers of rain so that the country seems to be in mourning.

We pass down into the plain, not unlike that of Salisbury and reach our billeting area at **Born.** The village is a very poor one and does not appear to me to be any better than those in France. The cottage rooms are the same, the crucifix over the bed and the beds themselves are too short. Most beds in the poorer class houses and, indeed, in the majority of the better class ones seem to be two sizes too short. I am not more than a middle-sized man yet even I have to tuck my legs, figuratively speaking, round my neck, and on top of the covering is a square eiderdown weighing about a ton, which if pulled round the neck uncovers the feet and eventually finds itself on the floor.

I am instructed to post examining guards at the main road leaving the village and proceed to a cottage to place the piquet in. On entering, the whole family flies upstairs and appears to be panic-stricken. In time they find we are not quite what they expected and come down one by one to find out what we want. My school French has been extremely useful in France and Belgium but my deepest regret is that I didn't learn German and it is with gesticulations that I make them understand my meaning.

17 December 1918

We march in the rain to **Honningen,** where we learn we are to remain for a few days. We are now high up again. The Company is rather scattered and I have seen them all safely into good billets. Our mess is in the house of a woodman, who can talk a certain amount of French. The rooms are decorated with antlers and sporting trophies of all kinds and he tells us that he will take us to 'hunt the stags' to which we readily acquiesce if we can spare the time.

18 and 19 December 1918

Heavy snow.

20 December 1918

We have collected from various houses all manner of wash-tubs and have fitted up a bath house and the men are enjoying a bath which has not fallen to their lot for sometime.

During the afternoon **Pentirth[?], Henderson** and I led by our guides and with our two servants wend our way into the hills in search of game. We call at the Keeper's Cottage in the forest. The house is a little chalet and hung inside with the usual trophies. The frau and children talk to us and show us the way to the Keeper who is felling Christmas trees as the season is approaching and evidently going to be kept up even though the land is being occupied. This fellow is a fine strapping man, too old for the army

Wild boar, Sus scrofa.

Roe buck, Capreolus capreolus.

and clad in Sherwood green with acorn epaulets to his typically military coat. On his head is a green homberg with the Imperial Eagle badge and at the side a blackcock's tail. He informs our guide that as it's snowing it will be difficult to obtain a shot as all game will take shelter in the thick undergrowth. The hills are covered with snow and stretch for miles in one large deer forest belonging to the state.

In many places we come across the spoor of wild boar [*Sus scrofa*] and roebuck, [*Capreolus capreolus*] and in two cases that of a large stag but our guide is correct and we see nothing. After wandering about for a few hours in the ever thickening snow, we trace our footsteps homewards and get lost in a blizzard. Our guide, however, finds a familiar landmark and we arrive at the mess in the dark. On the way back the old boy tells me in French that this part of the country was originally part of France though now part of Prussia and that the citizens of **Malmédy**, about three miles away, have sent a petition to the king of the Belgians to come under his rule. He says that the poor Kaiser was quite innocent but was ill advised by his scheming ministers.

21 December 1918
We arrive at **Hellenthal**.

We appear to be reaching the more civilized part of Germany. The houses in this little village are all black and white timbered buildings. The population is about 2,000.

22 December 1918
Last night I went out with another officer as we are not allowed to go singly and without revolvers, and looked the place over in the dark. Over the doorway of every house is an electric light and if you can imagine a well paint-

ed stage you have got it exactly; every minute I was half expecting my Lord so-and-so or Queen Elizabeth or a Court Jester to come bouncing out of the wings. There was no one about as the civilians are not allowed out after dark excepting those who have special permits. These were out in certain cases and wore wide-brimmed hombergs and long black cloaks.

23 December 1918

This is the worst march of all. Fifteen and a half miles in the pouring rain. I don't think we have been out in worse and everyone is drenched to the skin and water is running down our boots which are practically full of it. We arrive at hostel and the company, or the majority of the men, is in a great schoolroom.

Within five minutes everyone is running about the room in a clean, dry pair of pants and vest only, which they carried in the pack, whilst their clothes are drying round the two or three roaring stoves. In this condition they hold a topping concert, it is truly wonderful what the British Tommy can put up with.

24 December 1918

We arrive at our destination, the village of **Kommern/Commern** which is four miles from **Euskirchen.**

25 December 1918, Christmas Day

We have quite a cheery time though we do not hold our actual Christmas meals, these being reserved for January 1. We have heard that owing to lack of transport all the turkeys ordered for the Division from Paris have gone bad as they have been on a siding at **Namur** for over a week. Dance at night.

26 December 1918 to 3 January 1919

We have a programme of a little work in the morning and football during the afternoon. The evenings are generally taken up with concerts, whist drives, etc.

Kommern is only a small village and just accommodates ourselves and the A.S.C. All civilians are instructed to raise their hats to the officers. The time is now extended to 9pm and after that all civilians are to be within their houses.

Everyone is agreeably surprised with the way we are being received, that is with the greatest civility and even as if they enjoyed having us. The little Frau at my billet has always the kindest enquiries after me; our men are behaving themselves splendidly.

Gradually men are being demobilised and we shall soon not have any battalion left.

4 January 1919

Harrison and I visit **Cologne** which is about 30 kilometres from here.

After walking over the hill to **Micherincht,** a mining village, we catch the 7.30 train and pass the ticket collector who jumps up smartly to attention and does not ask for tickets; no fares are charged to the British. It is about an hour and a half's run to **Cologne** through flat and somewhat uninteresting country and on arrival we cross the square in which the Cathedral stands and enter the Dom Hotel - which is about the best in the city - and ask for a bed. The clerk informs us, in good English, that none are available but if we would fill in a form we shall get one at the Wimhof round the corner and we can then mess at the **Dom**. He informs us that we are guests of the Government of Germany and that we need only pay for meals.

Having found our hotel and after a good wash we look round the town and we are favourably impressed. The streets are full of English, Canadians, Australians, Americans, Belgians, French and of course Germans, many of whom are officers in uniform which appears strange.

The shop windows in the Hohe Strasse are full of gorgeous goods – at gorgeous prices – and there appears to be a plentiful supply of Iron Crosses on sale. Cigars are unlimited and the only thing that seems to be scarce are boots and these are indeed poor.

The scent shop is doing a roaring trade and of course everyone pays a visit to this even though it is patronising German goods and little packages of Eau de Cologne or Köln Wasser are sent to all quarters of the globe.

Our lunch is served by an attentive waiter who speaks English very well and who has of course lived in England, consists of goose and hot pickled cabbage (15 marks) and sawdust bread. We have been wise and brought a loaf, our own ration, a piece of which we place on the table much to the envy of the other officers in the rooms who have not been so wise – a little Rheine wine, no sweets as these are not allowed to be made. A small pot of Paté de foie Gras costs 12 marks. Our repast over, the Cathedral claims our attention and after having viewed the interior, a guide escorts us up the five hundred and eighteen steps to the top of the tower; through a room full of Goblin tapestries which were taken from the French long ago; through the belfry, from which we noted the famous Kayer bell has been removed to make ammunitions. (This bell weighed twenty six tons and the hammer alone was as large as a football.)

We peer out from the pinnacle – so high that we can hardly see the people down below – and see the Union Jack lazily floating over the **City of**

Cologne. The **Rhine,** a truly disappointing river at this place, winds its way through a flat, uninteresting plain and loses itself in the distance amongst the **Seven Sisters** and the **Drachenfels** further south.

During the afternoon we promenade the streets and at 5.30 find two seats at the opera. We had been there earlier but all the seats were full but we had been promised two returns if there were any. As luck would have it there were two and we obtained these in the face of a crowd clamouring for admission. **Harrison** says that my face did it - I hope he didn't mean to be rude.

The **Opera House** is huge, a little bigger than the Grand at Leeds and is of white stone inside. The ceiling is magnificently decorated. **'The Flying Dutchman'** is in progress.

At the interval the auditorium clears and the people parade in the prom-enade. This is a fine hall round the theatre and is almost as wide as the audi-torium itself. A thick red carpet is on the floor and the walls are hung with well-executed paintings of well-known characters, many of them from Shakespeare. People partake of a light supper in the café and during this German Red Cross nurses try to collect from, and in many cases succeed, British Officers money for German hospitals. This strikes me as being rather cool.

5 January 1919

Up at ten and attend service in the Cathedral which is packed and must hold thousands. The Square is black with people at the close.

We catch the train and arrive in **K(C)ommern** in time for tea.

6 to 16 January 1919

Time taken up with riding, cross-country running, bridge etc.

I learn that I am to be demobilised shortly and we have a farewell con-cert where my health is drunk and flattering speeches made, much to my consternation. I am handing my Company over to **Crabtree.**

We have exciting Hare Hunts. The Battalion forms a square of one com-pany at each side of nearly a mile wide and at a given signal, we close in and in doing so encircle a number of hares; on one occasion there are as many as sixteen but only three are caught. He who catches the hare is enti-tled to keep it. Everyone gets vastly excited and thoroughly enjoys the sport.

We have another farewell do. **Harrison** and I visit **Bonn** and we are not particularly impressed. We see the famous **Alter Zoll** and look up the **Rhine** which is just entering or rather just leaving its mountainous course.

A running brown hare, Lepus europaeus, after Reg Gammon.

18 January 1919
Waiting for my movement orders and I kill time for a few hours in riding to **Euskirchen**, a small town about seven miles from **Kommern.** It has a large barracks and nothing notable as far as I can see. It is the most English-looking town I have seen abroad.

19 to 27 January 1919
I leave the Batallion and conduct a party of a hundred men to **England**.

We spend a night and part of the next morning in **Düren** and I walk round and visit the museum and other principal buildings.

In one of the squares is or rather was a statue of **Wilhelm II.** This has been battered to pieces by the irate citizens of **Düren** and remnants lie about the square.

We billet the men for the night in the barracks and the officers stay in the Crown Hotel. **Düren** is a collecting place for demobilisation men and we catch the **Köln – Dunkirk** Express in the evening. I don't think I have used quite the word when I say express. During the whole journey to the base which occupies 72 hours the majority of the time is taken up with standing still.

The men are in loose boxes but they have charcoal fires in braziers whereas the poor officers are frozen to death in a dilapidated ambulance carriage. All the seats have been removed and we sit in state on the floor. Being nearly frozen we open our valises as well as we can without spilling all the contents and crawl into these, drawing close together and whiling away the time by either sleeping or playing bridge.

We pass through **Aix la Chapelle, Liege, Namur, Charleroi, Tournai, Lille** and finally arrive at **Dunkirk** where we proceed to that peculiar camp known as the Delousing Station where everyone has a bath. After this a little dinner at the Hotel does not come amiss and the following day, we arrive in **England**, entrain to **Prees Heath** in Shropshire and are finally demobilised [on 27 January 1919.]

~ ~ ~ ~ ~ ~ ~ ~ ~

As the sun sets over the City of Cologne so does it set over an epoch in my career

Four and a half years have slipped by since 1914 and I go back to make up those lost years - lost in one sense yet gained in another for have I not learnt to realise the sterling qualities in my friends, learnt a little more confidence in myself, gained a wider out-look on life and learnt that might is not always right? I draw a curtain over times in which there have been many glimpses of sunshine thro' the thunder clouds and I look forward to the Happiness of Peace.

The End

E. Raymond Hepper, Capt.

Postscript to the Diary:
The Life and Death of John (Jack) Valentine Heasman

AT the same time that Raymond Hepper was serving in the West Yorkshire Regiment in France, the brother of Cecilia Heasman, his wife-to-be, was also not far away near Amiens, where he was killed in 1916 while fighting with the Honourable Artillery Company.

THE HEASMAN FAMILY
Jack was the son of **George Valentine Heasman** 1861-1932 (my maternal Grandfather) who retired from a transatlantic cable-laying company c.1919, and **Ada Heasman** (née **Pailthorp** and my maternal Grandmother) who was born in 1864, died 2 January 1942 at Coniston aged 77 (details in Millom District, Vol.10b, page 1324).

    Jack was born at Leytonstone in 1896 and educated at Felsted School, an independent boarding/day school in Essex. On 31 May 1915, from his home address 10 Grosvenor Road, Westcliff-on-Sea, he joined the British

Jack Heasman with his parents and an aunt outside their home in Theydon Bois, Essex, 1915.

"Dear Sir,

"On 19th November last I had the sad news from the Matron of the 49th Casualty Clearing Hospital, France, that my dear only son Pte. J. V. Heasman 3605 had died on 17th of wounds received, and some time later I had the official notice through the War Office to the same effect. Since that time I have had no more information, and have rather expected to have had some acknowledgement of his services and his death from the regiment he had the honour, and my son felt so proud to belong, after having served for 5 years with the O.T.C. at Felsted School.

"As no doubt the records of the regiment show, he joined the 2nd Batt. at the end of May 1915 and went out with a draft from Orpington at the end of July last and joined the 1st Batt. later in France.

"I should be very pleased to know whether any of his personal belongings came back through the regiment or other source.

"Kindly accept my apologies for troubling you.

Yours faithfully,

G. V. Heasman"

No answer to this letter is recorded, and no personal effects have been retrieved. However, in due course his parents received his official war medals, which are now in the family's possession (see colour photographs page 124):

A visit by Nigel Hepper to the grave of Private Jack Heasman, May 2008. Photograph Brigadier Johnny Walker.

Silver War Medal; Obverse head, inscribed "GEORGIUS V BRITT. OMN: REX ET IND: IMP:

Reverse: Horse with naked rider, "1914 1918"; inscribed around the edge "3605 PTE. J. V. HEASMAN, H.A.C., INF."

Bronze Victory Medal; Obverse Winged Victory; Reverse wreath "The Great War for civilisation 1914-1919"; inscribed around the edge "3605 PTE. J. V. HEASMAN, H.A.C., INF."

A visit to Jack's grave
In 2007, during a visit to the National Archives at Kew, I was able to find details of Jack's service in the British Army and the whereabouts of his grave. He was buried in the Contay British Military Cemetery north east of Amiens, which I visited on 13 May 2008. There I placed a wooden cross with scarlet poppy at the foot of the inscribed headstone and I was photographed by Brigadier Johnny Walker, Guide of our Remembrance Tour (British Legion) – see colour section (page 123). I believe I am the only member of the Heasman/Hepper families – and possibly the only person ever – to make a pilgrimage to his grave. It was a moving experience for me.

F. Nigel Hepper

Chronology of the First World War

1914

28 June	Archduke Franz Ferdinand, heir to the Hapsburg thrones, assassinated at Sarajevo
28 July	Austria-Hungary declares war on Serbia
1 August	Germany declares war on Russia
3 August	Germany declares war on France
4 August	Germany invades Belgium and Great Britain declares war on Germany
20 August	British Expeditionary Force concentrated before Mauberge
23 August	Battle of Mons
5-9 September	Battle of the Marne
16 September	Trench warfare began on Aisne salient
12 Oct-11 Nov.	First Battle of Ypres
5 November	Britain declares war on Turkey
9 November	Sea Battle of Coronel (Chile): two German cruisers sink two British cruisers

1915

17 February	Germans start sea blockade of Britain
1 March	Allied fleets start sea blockade of Germany
25 April	Landing of ANZAC troops on Gallipoli Peninsula
22 Apr-25 May	Second Battle of Ypres
7 May	Germany first used gas
9-25 May	Battle of Aubers Ridge

1916

10-15 March	Battle of Neuve Chapelle
8 January	Evacuation of Gallipoli completed
21 February	Battle of Verdun began between German and French forces
31 May	Naval Battle of Jutland
5 June	Lord Kitchener drowns off Orkney when ship mined
1 July-13 Nov.	Battle of the Somme: 420,000 British casualties
15 September	Tanks first used by British
26 September	Allies capture Combles and Thiepval
6 December	Lloyd George forms War Cabinet; Joffre replaced by Nivelle

1917

1 February	Unrestricted submarine warfare begins
12 March	Revolution in Russia
6 April	USA declares war on Germany
9-14 April	Battle of Arras
10 April	Vimy Ridge taken by Canadians
3 May	Mutiny in sections of French army
15 May	Pétain replaced Nivelle
7 June	Messines Ridge taken by British
26 June	First American contingents arrive in France
31 July	Third Battle of Ypres
4 October	British victory on Passendaele Ridge
6-7 October	Bolsheviks come to power in Russia
23 October	French victory at Aisne
20 November	Hindenburg Line smashed during Battle of Cambrai
9 December	Allenby captures Jerusalem
15 December	Russo-German armistice signed

1918

21 March	German offensive against British opened on the Somme
21 Mar-4 Apr	Battle of Arras
9-25 April	Second German offensive against British
14 April	Foch appointed C.-in-C. Allied armies
23 April	British naval raid on Zeebrugge and Ostend
19 June	British Government introduces general rationing
15 July	Last German offensive against French halted
8 August	British, Australians and Canadians attack in front of Amiens
29 August	Allied victory at Amiens
26 September	General Allied offensive on Western Front began
9 November	Kaiser abdicates and escapes to Holland
11 November	Armistice signed by Germans
21 November	German High Seas Fleet impounded at Scapa Flow

1919

18 January	Peace Conference in Paris
21 June	German sailors scuttle High Seas Fleet in Scapa Flow

Index of Military Units

Mentioned in Captain E. Raymond Hepper's diary with at least one date. Excluding his own West Yorkshire Regiment 8th, 16th, 17th, 18th (except Leeds Pals 15th)

American Railway Engineers: 8.9.17

Army HQ (2nd): 14.10.17

Army HQ (5th): 4.11.17

Brigade 104th, 105th, 106th: 18.3.17

Cheshire Regiment: 17.6.16; 13.19.16; 25/26.11.16; 13.2.17; 3.3.17

Corps (VI) (Officers' Club): 16.10.18

Devonshire Regiment: 8.11.18

Division (17th): 26.11.17

Division (22nd): 18.3.17

Division (34th): 1.1.18

Division (35th): 26.11.17

Division (61st): 18.3.17

Durham Light Infantry (DLI): 31.1.16; 3.2.16; 11.3.16; 22.3.16; 20.4.16; 2.8.16; 24.8.16; 9.10.16; 12.10.16; 25/26.11.16; 2.3.17; 11.4.17; 14.4.17; 30.3.17; 19.5.17; 28.5.17; 8.8.17; 9.9.17

Gloucestershire Regiment (14th): 11.4.16; 2.6.16

Hampshire Regiment: 16.10.18

Highland Light Infantry (HLI): 12.3.16; 18.9.16; 19.9.16; 21.3.17; 19.5.17; 28.5.17; 8.8.17; 19.8.17

Indian Cavalry (Bengal Lancers; Poona Horse; 17th Lancers; 9th Hodson's Horse; 29th Lancers (Deccan Horse): 13.5.17

King Edward's Horse: 17.3.17

King's (Liverpool Regiment): 30.7.16

King's Own Yorkshire Light Infantry (KOYLI): 4.11.18; 6.11.18

King's Royal Rifle Corps (KRRC) (17th): 28.5.16; 11.6.16

Lancashire (as Lancaster) Fusiliers

(17th): 28.4.16; 25/26.11.16

Leeds Pals: see West Yorkshire Regiment (15th)

Lincolnshire Regiment (2nd): 25-27.3.16

Nottinghamshire & Derbyshire Regiment (as Notts & Derby; also as Sherwood Foresters): 5.5.16; 30.5.16

Royal Engineers (RE): 30.12.16; 2.3.17; 26.11.18

Royal Field Artillery (RFA) battery: 14.4.17; 26.11.18

Royal Flying Corps (RFC): 17-22.4.17; 10.10.17

Royal Scots (Lothian Regiment) (17th): 1.2.16; 22.3.16; 29.3.16; 16.9.16; 13.11.16; 19.12.16; 2.3.17; 14.4.17; 30.4.17; 19.5.17; 6.8.17; 8.8.17

Royal Warwickshire Regiment: 7.3.16; 21.3.17 onwards

Royal Welsh Fusiliers (9th): 20.2.16; 23.2.16

Sherwood Foresters: see Nottinghamshire & Derbyshire Regiment

South Wales Borderers (10th): 15.4.16

Warwicks: see Royal Warwickshire Regiment

'Welsh Guard Fusiliers': see Royal Welsh Fusiliers

West Yorkshire Regiment (15th): 5.7.16; 8.11.17; 5.12.17

Wiltshire Regiment: 23.2.16

Index of People

Mentioned in Capt. Raymond Hepper's Great War Diary. Military personnel with rank when known, also a few civilians. Date cited: day. month.year

Alexander, Sir R., 20.8.17
Allan, Capt., 21.3.17; 19.5.17; 21.5.17; 11-13.10.17
Andy the cook, 24.8.16
Atkinson, Lt. Col. F. St. J., 1.2.16; 2-3.11.16

Banks, 3.9.16; 18.9.16
Battishill, Lieut., 2.11.16; 31.8.17; 22.9.17; 10.12.17
Bell, Capt., 19.3.16; 16.4.17; 31.8.17
Bell's groom, 21.3.17
Bell, Rev/Padre, 22.7.16 as Padre
Best, 7.7.16
Bingham, Cyril, 15.10.17
Blower, Cpl., 31.5.16; 29.7.16
Bouelin, interpreter, 6.2.17; 8.2.17
Box, Sgt., 2.11.16
Braithwaite, 30.12.16
Burley, Sgt., 28.3.16
Butler, 18.2.16; 21.2.18

Canterbury, Archbishop of (Davidson), 22.5.16
Churchill, Winston, 11.5.16
Cleghorn, Lieut. RE, 2-3.11.16
Cohen, 4.2.16; 21.5.17; 23.7.17
Colbeck, 1.4.16; 14.4.16; 2.12.17
Connaught, Prince Arthur of, 9.2.16
Crabtree, 5.1.19
Crawford, 20.2.16; 1.4.16
Cross, 10.2.16

Davidson, Randall Thomas see Canterbury, Archbishop
Dehaene, 1.1.18

DeLissa, 31.12.16
DeWitt, 25.4.16; 19.1.17; 17.2.17
Dye, Sgt., 14.9.16
Dykes, 29.7.16

Eadie, 31.12.16
Euselene, interpreter, 31.8.16; 15.3.17; 21.3.17; 11-13.10.17
Evans, 7.12.17; 10.12.17
Ewing, 11.6.16

Ffoulkes, 22.3.16
Forshaw, 26.8.16
Fortune, Col., 30.10.17
Fotherby, 2.12.18
Frank, Gen., 20.8.17
Fricker, Eric, 19.3.16; 23.6.16
Fry, 7.12.17; 10.12.17

Garburt, 10.12.17
Garlic, 6.12.17
Gaudy, 16.10.18
Gibbs, Philip, 28.8.16
Gill, Maj., 19.3.16; 8.11.17; 7.12.17; 10.12.17
Greig, 15.3.17

Hadow, 1.3.17; 29.5.17
Haig, Sir Douglas, 9.2.16
Hakin, Gen., 15.2.16
Haldane, Gen., 19.12.16
Hall, Maj., 24.3.16; 13.2.17
Hamilton, 9.3.16
Hampden, Brig.-Gen. Lord, 13.11.18
Hannay, Canon, 1.2.16
Hardaker, 24.3.16

Harris, 25.4.16
Harris, servant, 19.12.16
Harrison, 25.10.18; 20.11.18; 4.1.19
Havernas, Compt de, 8.2.17
Hayton, Sgt., 16.2.16
Heathcote, Col., 8.9.17
Heaton, 20.4.16
Hemsley, Sgt., 30.11.17
Henderson, 20.11.18
Hersch, Philip, VC, 1.1.18
Hitchen, 6.6.16
Hoggett, 16.6.16
Houston, 26.10.16
Huffam, Capt., 2.2.16; 3.3.16
Hunter, servant, 12.7.16

Jackson, 7.4.16
Jenkinson (Jenkins?), 29.10.16; 17.3.17; 13.9.17

Kavanagh, 6.6.16
Keeton, Lieut., 30.7.16
Kelly, 30.12.16
Kitchener, Lord, 11.2.16

Lachan, 31.8.17
Landon, Gen., 8.7.17; 8.2.17
Lawton, 7.12.17; 9.12.17
Lyne, Sgt., 29.6.16

Marshall, 8.3.16; 17.4.16
Mason, 28.2.16; 19.3.16; 24.3.16
Martin, 12.9.16
May, Sgt., 2.11.16
MCate, 25.12.17
McDonald, cook, 3.4.17
McKnight, 13.11.16
McPake, 31.12.16
Merindan?, ADC, 20.8.17; 23.9.17
Merindan?, Gen., 19.10.17
Midgley, B., 9.6.16
Millar, Pte., 14.9.16
Moore, Col., 12.7.16
Moreland, Gen., 22.4.17; 22.9.17
Mundy, 25.11.16

Murray, 8.9.17

Nesbit 6.11.18
Newman, Col. 21.3.17
Norman (?N.Wootton), 9.4.16

Oates, 7.8.11.18; 16.11.18
O'Donnell, Gen., 14.5.17
O'Leary, Michael, 19.3.16

Padre, see Bell.
Parker, 28.3.16
Penney (?Pinney), Gen., 6.4.16; 22.8.16
Percival, 7.4.16
Pentirth, 20.12.18
Pollard, Col., 1.2.16
Priquant, Capt., 31.8.17

Redman, 2.2.16; 3.3.16; 2.4.18
Rich, Jimmy, 26.10.18
Robespierre, 29.10.16
Robertshaw, servant, 8.11.18
Robinson, Sgt., 14.9.16; 21?12.17
Rodley, servant, 20.3.17; 15.4.17; 12.8.17
Rose, Capt., 18.2.16; 1.4.16; 9.6.16; 6-14.3.17; 17.3.17; 31.8.17
Ross, 29.8.16; 6.2.17; 8.2.17; 22.2.17; 21.3.17; 31.8.17
Rutherford, Lieut., 2.11.16
Rycroft, Col., 21.3.17; 14.4.17; 8.9.17; 9.10.17; 30.10.17

Shield, 7.4.16
Singer, interpreter, 16.6.16
Sowry, 31.8.17
Stansfield, 6.1.18
Stead, C., Sgt.-Maj., 8.11.18
Stead, Willy, 26.8.16
Styche, 9.3.16
Sutherland, 29.6.16

Tadman, Adj., 31.8.17
Thirau, Joseph (and junior), 25.11.18

Index of Place Names

Modified transcriptions from difficult hand-writing, and first-mentioned date in Diary with day.month.year.

N.B. some names relate to temporary camps and earthworks.

(?) = place not located and not entered on maps 1-8 (see pages 57-63).

Abbéville, 27.9.17

Acq, 5.12.17

Agicourt, 2.6.17; 1.9.17; 16.9.17

Agnez-lès-Duisans, 9.10.17

Aire, 15.2.16

Aizecourt-le-Haut, 2.6.17

Albert, 12.7.16; 29.8.16

Amiens,   29.8.16; 20.8.17; 23.9.17; 26.9.17

Annéquin, 19.3.16

Anthee (?), 7.7.16

Antheux, 29.8.16

Armentières, 24.3.16

Arneke, 14.10.17; 16.10.17

Arras, 28.6.16; 2.9.16; 9.9.16; 18.9.16; 20.9.16; 26.9.16; 29.10.16; 19.12.16; 9.10.17; 1.1.18

Arrowhead copse, 18.8.16

Athies, 21.3.17

Aubigny, 26.9.16

Auchy, 19.3.16

Avesnes-le-Comte, 3.9.16; 7.9.16

Bac St Maur, 27.3.16

Barlin, 4.12.17

Baudringhem, 7.2.16

Belle Croix, 7.2.16

Bellenglise, 11.4.17

Bernafay South Trench (?), 29.7.16; 30.7.16; Wood (?) 22.7.16

Bernaville, 29.8.16

Béthune, 19.3.16; 29.4.16; 16.6.16

Beuvry, 19.3.16

Bévillers, 16.10.18

Billone Wood (?), 11.7.16; 18.8.16

Boeseghem, 9.2.16

Boisleux, 1.1.18

Boulogne,   4.2.16; 26.9.16; 8.10.16; 27.9,17; 8.10.17; 16.10.18

Bousignies, 18.11.18

Brielen, 26.11.17

Briquetesil, 29.7.16

Broussig Bois(?), 28.2.17

Buchy, 3.2.16

Bullencourt, 22.12.17

Bussu, 21.5.17

Caftet wood, 22.7.16; 29.7.16; 31.7.16; 18.8.16

Caix, 22.2.17; 24.2.17; 15.3.17

Calais, 4.2.16

Calonne, 19.3.16; 22.3.16; 3.5.16

Cambrai, 16.10.18

Camp des Ballons (?), 24.2.17

Campagne, 4.2.16

Canaples(?), 29.8.16

Carnières, 16.10.18

Carnoy valley, 12.7.16

Casement Trench (?), 29.7.16; 27.8.16

Cassell, 14.10.17

Caterpillar Valley (?), 22.7.16

Caulaincourt, 23.4.17

Cavigny Farm, 21.3.17; 23.4.17

Celestine, Bois de (?),   10-11.7.16; 28.8.16

Cepy (?), 30.4.17

Champagne Trench (?), 24.8.16

Chapigny Farm, 10.3.16

Chapois, 27.11.18

Charleroi, 19-27.1.19

Neuve Chapelle, 10.3.16; 23.4.16; 11.5.16

Nieppe, Forêt de, 18.2.16; 23.3.16; 23-26.5.16

Obies, 8.11.18
Oise, 13.2.16
Omiécourt, 18.3.17; 20-21.3.17
Omignon, R., 10-11.4.17
Orsiuval (?), 5.11.18
Ourthe, R., 11.12.18
Outrebois, 7.2.17
Ovillers, 5.7.16

Pacault, 16.3.16
Paradis, 14.3.16; 3.5.16
Pargny, 21.3.17
Péronne, 21.3.17; 19.5.17; 8.9.17; 26.9.17
Petit Marais, 6.11.18
Picquigny, 11.8.16; 8.2.17
Pilken Ridge, 18.10.17
Pitt Camp, 8.11.17
Pont du Jour (?), 29.10.16
Poona Camp (?), 27.10.17
Poperinghe, 4.11.17
Porchester Camp (?), 8.11.17
Poteau, 16.12.18
Pozières, 2.8.16
Prees Heath (Shropshire), 19-27.1.19
Proven, 16.10.17; 27.10.17; 1.11.17; 8.11.17
Prusle (?), 21.3.17
Puisieux/Puzeaux (?), 21.3.17
Punchy, 21.3.17

Quene-au-Leu (Cheneau Loup) (?), 8.11.18

Racquinhem, 7.2.16
Raileau Mill (?), 23.5.17
Rebreuve Chateau (?), 7.2.17
Rhine, R., 4.1.19; 6-16.1.19
Richebourg, 6.5.16; 11.5.16
Riez Bailleul, 27.2.16

Roclincourt, 16.9.16; 18.9.16; 29.10.16
Roisel, 20.8.17
Ronssoy, 20.8.17
Rosières, 26.2.17; 6-14.3.17; 17.3.17; 21.3.17
Rouen, 3.2.16
Roye, 15.3.17; 17.3.17
Rudbroreck, 14-15.10.17
Rudbourek (see Rudbroreck)
Rue-des-Vignes, 29.5.17
Ruesnes, 5.11.18

Sailly, 3.4.16; 8.4.16
St Christ, 21.3.17; 10.4.17
St Helene salient (?), 16.4.17
St Martius Camp, (Boulogne), 16.10.18
St Nicholas (Arras), 10.7.16
St Pol, 3.12.16
St Quentin, 11.4.17
St Sylvestre Capell (?), 15.10.17
St Vincent (?), 18.2.16
Sandpit Valley (?), 1,2.8.16; 16.8.16
Serre, 5.7.16
Silesia Trench (?), 23.8.16
Solesmes, 16.10.18; 3.11.18; 27.11.18
Somme, R., 9-10.7.16; 11.8.16; 6.2.17; 8.2.17; 10.2.17; 13.2.17; 21.3.17; 10.4.17; 27.9.17
Sorrel le Grand, 21.5.17
Sous le Bois (?), 10.11.18
Spontin, 26.11.18
Station Redoubt (?), 22.12.17
Steenbecque, 12.5.16
Sunday Avenue, Arras, 10.9.16; 26.9.16
Sus St Leger, 31.8.16

Talus, Bois de (?), 12.7.16; 27.8.16
Tayompret (?), 7.11.18
Templeux la Fosse, 2.6.17
Tertry, 23.4.17
Thelus, 11.9.16
Thiepval, 5.7.16
Thieushouck, 1.12.17
Thouin/Thuin, 19.11.18; 20.11.18

Tir, Champ de (?), 23.3.16
Tournai, 19-27.1.19
Trônes Wood, 12.7.16
Tronquoy, 11.4.17

Vendricourt, Chateau de (?), 11.4.17
Vermand, 21.3.17; 10.4.17; 30.4.17; 12.5.17
Victoria Street (?), 2-3.11.16
Vielsalm, 14.12.18
Vignacourt, 8.2.17; 17.2.17
Villers-Guislain, 23.5.17; 24.5.17; 29.5.17; 3.6.17; 8.9.17
Vis-en-Artois, 1.1.18

Wardrecques, 7.2.16
Wancourt, 1.1.18
Warnant, 25.11.18
Warreimont, Bois de, 5.7.16
Waterlot farm (?), 28.8.16; 22.7.16
Wednesday Avenue (?), 16.9.16
Willerval, 11.9.16
Wood 15 (?), 19.10.17; 1.11.17

Ypres, 26.11.16; 21.3.17; 9.10.17
Yvoir, 26.11.18
Yz(s)eux, 8.2.17

Zoomer Bloom, 20.10.17;

Further Reading

Arthur, Max, in association with the Imperial War Museum, 2002, *Forgotten Voices of the Great War*, London: Random House Group.

Hart, Peter, 2005, *The Somme,* London: Weidenfelt & Nicholson.

Holmes, Richard, 1999, *The Western Front,* London: BBC Worldwide

Kipling, Rudyard, 1923, *The Irish Guards in the Great War*, 2 vols. 1st Battalion; 2nd Battalion, London. Second edition, 1997; 2nd Battalion, Staplehurst: Spellmount Ltd.

Lynch, E. D. F. (edited by Will Davies), 2006, *Somme Mud: Experiences of an Infantryman in France, 1916-1919,* London: Bantam Books (Random House)

Man, John, 1998, *The War to End Wars 1914-18,* London: Readers' Digest Association

Osman, A. H., *Pigeons in the Great War: a complete history of the carrier pigeon service during the Great War 1914 to 1918,* London: Racing Pigeon Publishing.

Neillands, Robin, 2004, *The Old Contempibles: The British Expeditionary Force, 1914*, London: John Murray